# GENESIS
## FOUNDATION BOOK OF THE BIBLE

### MIKE MAZZALONGO

# TEACHER'S GUIDE

BIBLETALK.TV

**DOWNLOAD
OUR APP**

# Genesis
## *Foundation Book of the Bible*

---

**Mike Mazzalongo**

A 50-lesson series that covers all 50 chapters of Genesis. From creation to the flood and on to Abraham finishing with Joseph in Egypt. A complete study of the first book in the Bible.

## bibletalk.tv/genesis

**Main Resource:**
The Genesis Record
Dr. Henry Morris

**Teacher Guide created by David Laton, D.Min.**
2020

# Table of Contents

# Overall Teaching Strategy

It is recommended that teachers use a combination of informal lecture and guided discussion to present these lessons. There are discussion questions associated with each lesson that teachers may use and/or supplement with their own questions.

It is recommended that teachers have students view the associated video or read the text for the lesson. This helps students come to the class ready to discuss the lesson and to formulate questions of their own. Teachers should begin the class with a review of key points from the video/text before starting the discussion.

Begin each lesson with appropriate introductory statements that help students focus on the lesson. Teachers should also provide a brief summary of the previous lesson and an overview of key points of the new lesson. This helps students see the ongoing narrative of scripture.

Conclude the lesson by summarizing or having students summarize the information from their notes. It is also helpful to ask questions from the lesson to determine that students grasp the concepts. Asking questions in this manner serves as an assessment to ensure objectives are met.

Challenge students with a call to action by applying this information to their lives in order to help them grow spiritually and help others to do so as well. This can be accomplished by asking students how this information relates to their spiritual development at this time and moving forward.

For more information on teaching adults, please visit:
**https://bibletalk.tv/101/teaching**

A student workbook is also available for this series:
**https://bibletalk.tv/workbooks/genesis**

# Lesson #1 – Book of Origins

### Teaching Strategy

The focus of this lesson is to introduce information and events whose origins are found in the book of Genesis. Of special note in this lesson is the importance of Genesis as foundational for our faith and how Genesis is based on inspiration, not myth or analogy.

### Student Learning Outcomes

- **Know**: Understand how Genesis builds faith as an inspired work of God.

- **Feel**: Develop an awareness of the role Genesis plays in God's overall plan for man.

- **Do**: Use the information gained from Genesis to strengthen our faith.

### Support

- Series – Genesis – Foundational Book of the Bible (Mike Mazzalongo)

- Video – Lesson 1 – Book of Origins

- Student Note Guide for Lesson 1

### Body of the Lesson

1.1     Importance of the Book of Genesis
1.2     The "Origins" of Genesis
1.3     Genesis and the Bible

## Discussion Questions

Below are suggested questions to use during the guided discussion portion of the lesson. There are also suggested responses to questions to help students grasp the various concepts. These are provided to assist the discussion and are not considered as "right or wrong" responses.

## 1. Discuss the concept of inspiration and how Genesis supports this concept.

In the context of scripture, inspiration takes on several forms. The first is, "divine" origin. The original language means, "God breathed." When this form is used, the expression is "inspired of God" (2 Timothy 3:16). Another term is "inspiration of the Bible" showing how God used prophetic agents such as prophets (Hebrews 1:1). The prophets were speaking or writing but the words were God's. The inspiration of human writers does not mean they were "transcribers" but were using their human personalities and experiences in the process. They used firsthand knowledge, the aid of eyewitnesses and written sources to compose scripture (Luke 1:1-4). This was done under the guidance of the Holy Spirit. The understanding of scripture as inspired by God, however it is produced, shows the authoritative nature of scripture. It is the final word on all things religious.

Genesis provides the authoritative record of creation, man's fall and the foundation for God's plan for mankind's reconciliation following sin. If one is unable to believe in the inspiration of Genesis, then all of scripture is compromised.

**2. Review each of the following origins found in Genesis and be prepared to discuss its importance to man's understanding of God and His role with humanity. Origins of:**

- The universe
- The earth and all its elements
- Life in the form of plants and animals
- Man
- Marriage
- Evil
- Language
- Culture, Government and nations
- Religion
- God's chosen people

The intent of this question is to see how Genesis is foundational to man's understanding of God and creation. As mankind began to populate the earth and move further away from his relationship with God, more questions arose as to how creation occurred and why. Man has formulated many theories, but these do not answer the core question of how it all began. Genesis provides that information for us. As man has searched, he has discovered the reliable truth of Genesis.

### 3. Provide examples of how Genesis impacts all of scripture.

Historical figures from Genesis are seen throughout history demonstrating their role and purpose in God's plan.

Genesis is quoted throughout the New Testament.

All New Testament authors as well as Jesus refer to passages from Genesis 1 to 11.

### 4. How can you use this lesson to grow spiritually and help others come into a relationship with Jesus?

Understanding that the inspiration of Genesis is foundational to building our faith in the legitimacy of all scripture. Without this understanding we are unable to believe any other part of the Bible. The overwhelming evidence from historical figures, events and locations help validate the authenticity of statements made in Genesis. We can use this information as we teach others of the authority of scriptures for our salvation and behavior as citizens of God's Kingdom.

# Lesson #2 – Authorship and Division of Genesis

## Teaching Strategy

The focus of this lesson is on the authorship and divisions of Genesis. Of special note in this lesson is an overview of various theories of authorship with emphasis on the inspiration and structure of Genesis.

## Student Learning Outcomes

- **Know**: Identify why we believe that Moses is the author of Genesis and how Genesis is structured.

- **Feel**: Defend Moses as the author of Genesis.

- **Do**: Use the information gained from Genesis to strengthen our faith.

## Support

- Series – Genesis – Foundational Book of the Bible (Mike Mazzalongo)

- Video – Lesson 2 – Authorship and Division of Genesis

- Student Note Guide for Lesson 2

## Body of the Lesson

1.1     Authorship of Genesis
1.2     Divisions of Genesis
1.3     Application to our faith and continued spiritual growth

# Discussion Questions

Below are suggested questions to use during the guided discussion portion of the lesson. There are also suggested responses to questions to help students grasp the various concepts. These are provided to assist the discussion and are not considered as "right or wrong" responses.

**1. Explain the difference between "higher critics" and "textual scholars" and state why higher criticism is the weaker of the two methods for interpreting scripture.**

- The interpretation method of higher critics looks at scripture from the context of literature, religion and social customs of that period. This position holds that scripture is not inspired but rather a compilation of legends, stories and traditions. It denies the divine inspiration of Genesis.

- The interpretational method of textual scholars seeks to determine meaning from studying the text and related manuscripts. This method does not consider external phenomena or social stimulus as critical to interpretation. One of the problems some have in accepting the textual scholar's view is that they see variations in events in Genesis from other texts as the same level of validity as scripture itself.
  A strength of this method is that later discoveries from science, archeological efforts and scholarly reviews have shown the content of Genesis to be accurate.

**2. Summarize the three theories for the authorship of Genesis and defend why Moses is the author.**

- **A group of writers after Moses** – This view suggests that several writers compiled various stories and traditions from the region and society of the time. These were compiled between 700 and 400 BC. Moses is then credited as the author to provide this view with authority and authenticity.

- **Moses as the author** – This is a traditional view stating that Moses authored the first 5 books of the Old Testament (Pentateuch). It states that Moses received direct revelation from God, information from oral traditions and collected written records of the past and organized them into a book under the guidance of the Holy Spirit. Although possible and plausible, this is not the normal way God provides inspiration for communicating His will.

- **Moses as compiler and editor** – This holds that Moses compiled written records preserved from the patriarchs.  The records were preserved, and Moses collected these and edited them under that guidance of the Holy Spirit.

Although each of these theories presents insights into possible authorship, the theory that it was a group of writers has been refuted by modern scholars.   The other two with Moses as the author is the most likely scenario.

## 3. Summarize the two overview divisions of Genesis.

- **Chapters 1-11** – God creates the world and man.  Explains how sin came into existence and how nations, governments, language and other elements of life and society began.
- **Chapters 12-50** – Explains how God formed His people through His choice and promise to Abram (Abraham) and through this people worked out His plan to redeem mankind.

## 4. Explain the generational division of Genesis.

This structural view of Genesis shows how each generation from Adam to Jacob describes the spread of mankind in the world and God's role in working out His plan to save mankind through these people.

## 5. What is the key point from each of the following references from Genesis by Jesus and their significance?

- **Matthew 19:4-5; Mark 10:6-7** – God instituting marriage and the family.

- **Matthew 23:35; Luke 11:51** – Jesus references Abel as a historical, righteous person

- **Matthew 24:37-39** – Jesus comparing His return to the flood and how many will be unprepared.

- **Mark 13:19** – Jesus referring to God creating the world.

- **John 8:44** – The devil is a liar and a murderer "from the beginning".

The significance of Jesus referring to Genesis is that (1) Jesus' teaching of God the Father as the creator of the world and mankind. (2) Jesus identifying the presence and character of the devil and bringing evil into the world. (3) Jesus identifying events and individuals from scripture showing their real existence in history.

## 6. How can you use this lesson to grow spiritually and help others come into a relationship with Jesus?

Genesis is inspired scripture and serves as a foundation for our faith and continued spiritual growth. It also serves as a foundation point from which we can teach others about God's promise to redeem us from sin (Genesis 3:15).

# Lesson 3 – Foundational Verse of the Bible

## Teaching Strategy

The focus of this lesson is to review the first verse of Genesis as foundational to scripture. Of special note in this lesson is how Genesis 1:1 refutes various incorrect philosophies about God, creation, man's role and evolution.

## Student Learning Outcomes

- **Know**: Understand the importance of Genesis 1:1 as foundational to our faith.

- **Feel**: Appreciate the role Genesis 1:1 plays in establishing the supremacy of God.

- **Do**: Use the information gained from Genesis to strengthen our faith.

## Support

- Series – Genesis – Foundational Book of the Bible (Mike Mazzalongo)

- Video – Lesson 3 – The Foundational Verse of the Bible

- Student Note Guide for Lesson 3

## Body of the Lesson

1.1     Genesis 1:1 as a foundational verse
1.2     Genesis 1:1 refutes philosophies
1.3     The words in Genesis 1:1
1.4     Genesis 1:1 time, space, and matter
1.5     Lessons

# Discussion Questions

Below are suggested questions to use during the guided discussion portion of the lesson. There are also suggested responses to questions to help students grasp the various concepts. These are provided to assist the discussion and are not considered as "right or wrong" responses.

## 1. Explain the concept of a foundation and how Genesis 1:1 fulfills this role.

A foundation is the base upon which something is built. Genesis 1:1 sets the foundation of the supremacy of God over all things by creating all elements of our existence including the heavens, the earth and all that is contained therein. Without this established supreme identity and role of God, all other scripture would be invalid. It does not prove the existence of God, but simply establishes who He is and what He has done.

As an additional thought, it is the basis for God's statement to Moses in Exodus 3:14; "God said to Moses, "I Am Who I Am." And He said, "Say this to the people of Israel: "I Am has sent me to you." The expression "I Am" indicates a being with no beginning or end. Jesus also expressed His relationship as part of the Godhead in John 8:58, "Jesus said to them, "Truly, Truly, I say to you, before Abraham was, I am." (ESV)

## 2. Review each of the philosophies below and discuss how Genesis 1:1 refutes them.

**Atheism** – states there is no God. Genesis 1:1 simply states that God created the heavens and the earth. Atheism is unable to prove the nonexistence of God.

**Pantheism** – God is in everything. Genesis 1:1 states that God created everything. God is separate and superior to His creation. He existed before and after creation.

**Polytheism** – Teaches the multiplicity of God. Many ancient people and some modern societies hold to a variety of gods with various roles and powers. Genesis 1:1 simply states there is one God that created all things and is superior to all things.

**Materialism** – States that matter is eternal and is the only thing that exists. Genesis 1:1 states that matter had a beginning. At some point it did not exist until God spoke it into existence. Materialism cannot prove its eternal existence.

**Dualism** – States that there are two powers at work; good and evil and their interaction is responsible for all we see. Genesis 1:1 states that what we see was created by God and was created as, "Good." Evil has never been at the same level as God.

**Humanism** – Teaches that man is the ultimate reality. There is nothing higher or nobler than man. Genesis 1:1 teaches that God, not man, is the ultimate reality since God existed before man and is the creator of man.

**Evolution** – Teaches that time and chance working on eternal matter is responsible for the universe and all of creation. Genesis 1:1 says that in the beginning (a specific time), God created (not chance) the heavens and the earth. Genesis then goes on to state how God created our world and all within it. God intentionally and with a plan created the heavens and earth as fully developed.

## 3. Break down each word from Genesis 1:1 into its respective meaning and state the importance of the complete sentence.

**Note:** Consider having each student explain these words from their own understanding.

- God
- Created
- Heaven
- Earth
- In the beginning

Together these words form the foundation of our faith and confidence in God as our creator and savior.

## 4. Explain how Genesis 1:1 describes the matter, time, and space components.

Created refers to the unique work of God. It means to call into existence from nothing. Before creation there was no matter, time or space. When God created heaven, He created the element of space. Heavens refers to the place where stars, planets and other elements are located. When He created the element of earth, He created the element of matter. Initially it was not shaped but simply existed. Later He would form the world as we know it. When God performed the actions of creation, He created the element of time. The expression, "In the beginning" indicates a start to time.

## 5. What is the relationship between Genesis 1:1 and Genesis 2:4?

Genesis 1:1 states the action taken by God. Genesis 2:4 summarizes the detail contained within God's actions from Genesis 1:1 and serves as a transition into the detail of the creation of man and his environment.

As a side note, Genesis 2:15 states that God placed man in the garden to work it and keep it. This is significant in that it shows the reason why God created man and our role today as servants of our Lord.

## 6. How can you use this lesson to grow spiritually and help others come into a relationship with Jesus?

It is normal for us to wonder how things began. God provides the answer in Genesis 1:1 and following. He spoke creation into existence. This simple statement forms the foundation of our faith in God as our creator and savior. Genesis goes on to explain how sin entered the world but that because of God's love, He provided a way for us to be reconciled. He stated this in Genesis 3:15. As we reach out to others to show them our Lord, we can speak with authority from God's word concerning His supremacy over all things and all philosophies.

# Lesson 4 – Old Earth vs. Young Earth

## Teaching Strategy

The focus of this lesson is on the differences between the old earth view and young earth view. Of special note in this lesson is how the old earth view is not supported by logic, observation or revelation. Furthermore, this lesson explains how the young earth view as described in the creation record from Genesis is valid and can be defended.

## Student Learning Outcomes

- **Know**: Understand the old word view and young earth view.

- **Feel**: Defend the validity of the young world view and its support for the record of creation from Genesis.

- **Do**: Use the information gained from Genesis to strengthen our faith.

## Support

- Series – Genesis – Foundational Book of the Bible (Mike Mazzalongo)

- Video – Lesson 4 – Old Earth Vs. Young Earth

- Student Note Guide for Lesson 4

## Body of the Lesson

1.1     The old earth view
1.2     The young earth view
1.3     Lessons

# Discussion Questions

Below are suggested questions to use during the guided discussion portion of the lesson. There are also suggested responses to questions to help students grasp the various concepts. These are provided to assist the discussion and are not considered as "right or wrong" responses.

## 1. Describe the "old earth view" and summarize the threats to the validity of this view.

A view that directly supports the evolutionist philosophy that matter is eternal, was affected in some way, and through time and change the earth evolved to become what it is. The time element refers to a period that is millions to billions of years long beginning with some sort of phenomena described by many as the "big bang(s)".

This view has several problems: (1) It does not support the normal scientific process of observing fact and developing a theory to explain it. Rather, it presents a theory and then looks for or develops evidence. (2) The evidence presented is unproven. Although fossils exist showing all forms of life, extinct and otherwise, it does not show or support a timeline offered by those that hold this view. (3) Something cannot come from nothing. It must be created at some point. (4) Matter is not eternal. (5) The possibility of random chance bringing about the complexity of even the simplest form of life is beyond the range of possibility. (6) Geological facts do not support this view. Complex forms of life are found in the geological formations where only simple forms of life are expected to be located. (7) There are no fossil records showing the evolutionary progress among and between species (no "missing link").

## 2. Describe the "young earth view" and summarize why this is a valid view.

A view that supports that an all-powerful and wise being created the universe which reflects His complexity, power and wisdom is logical and possible. This view holds that the earth is between 5,000 to 10,000 years old.

This view is valid based on several observable views: (1) Fully developed and functional forms of life appear simultaneously throughout geological evidence as described by the creation record. (2) There are no links between one form of life and another, just as creation records. (3) Scientific dating processes do not go beyond 60,000 years. (4) The Bible contains genealogical records that list patriarchs from Adam through Moses and Christ which reflects no more than 8,000 years of history.

### 3. How can you use this lesson to grow spiritually and help others come into a relationship with Jesus?

We can have confidence that God's word is true in all ways, beginning with creation until the present time as we live out our faith today. We see where God is faithful to His promises so we can have confidence in His promise of salvation through Christ. As we reach out to others to help them develop their relationship with Jesus, we can show them through logic, observation and revelation that God's word is true.

# Lesson 5 – The Gap Theory in Creationism

## Teaching Strategy

The focus of this lesson is to focus on the creation of our universe by God. Of special note in this lesson is the fallacy of the perspective that there was a gap in time between God's initial creation and the six days of creation that followed.

## Student Learning Outcomes

- **Know**: Understand the process of creation as recorded in Genesis 1.

- **Feel**: Defend the process of creation as recorded in Genesis 1.

- **Do**: Use the information gained from Genesis to strengthen our faith.

## Support

- Series – Genesis – Foundational Book of the Bible (Mike Mazzalongo)

- Video – Lesson 5 – The Gap Theory in Creationism

- Student Note Guide for Lesson 5

## Body of the Lesson

1.1     The Gap Theory
1.2     Exegesis of Genesis 1:2
1.3     Lessons

# Discussion Questions

Below are suggested questions to use during the guided discussion portion of the lesson. There are also suggested responses to questions to help students grasp the various concepts. These are provided to assist the discussion and are not considered as "right or wrong" responses.

## 1. Summarize the main elements of the Gap theory.

This theory contends that there was a tremendous gap in time between Genesis 1:1 and Genesis 1:2. During this time Satan rebelled which led to the earth being destroyed and left blank and void. This is done to explain the alleged billions of years of fossils being built up. Verse 2 begins after this gap where God "recreates" the world.

## 2. Summarize the main problems with the Gap Theory.

Scientific – A cataclysmic destruction of the earth would have destroyed all evidence, especially fossil evidence of a previous creation.

Biblical – Several scriptures show that the Gap Theory is not valid. Romans 5:12, 1 Corinthians 15:21, and Romans 6:23.

## 3. Explain how Genesis 1:2 shows that God's creative activities were not disrupted by Satan's rebellion as described by the Gap Theory.

Moses records the activities with the conjunction, "and" showing continuous activities.

<u>And</u> the earth was formless <u>and</u> void (simple space and matter brought into existence), and darkness was on the face of the deep (this is an additional description of the condition of the earth with time, space and matter having been created). Matter had not yet been energized.

"...the Spirit of God moved over the surface of the waters."  The Holy Spirit, as part of the Godhead, brings energy to creation resulting in form. Following this statement we see the actions of God continuing to create until He rested on the seventh day.

**4. How can you use this lesson to grow spiritually and help others come into a relationship with Jesus?**

God offers us a simple explanation of His creation in Genesis 1. Sinful man tries to complicate or explain it away which weakens our faith. The attempt to weaken our faith is one of the strategies Satan uses to keep us from knowing and obeying God. We must simply accept God's word as truth, even if we don't fully understand it. God will grant us understanding as He wills. If we do not accept God's account of creation, we then undermine the truthfulness of all other scripture, especially His promise to reconcile us to Him through Jesus.

# Lesson 6 – The Day-Age Theory of Creation

## Teaching Strategy

The focus of this lesson is to understand the Day-Age theory of creation. Of special note in this lesson are the fallacies of this theory and how God spoke the cycle of life into existence.

## Student Learning Outcomes

- **Know**: Understand how Genesis builds faith as in inspired work of God.

- **Feel**: Develop an awareness of the role Genesis plays in God's overall plan for man.

- **Do**: Use the information gained from Genesis to strengthen our faith.

## Support

- Series – Genesis – Foundational Book of the Bible (Mike Mazzalongo)

- Video – Lesson 6 – The Day/Age Theory of Creation

- Student Note Guide for Lesson 6

## Body of the Lesson

1.1    Summary of the Day/Age theory
1.2    The creation of light
1.3    Lessons

# Discussion Questions

Below are suggested questions to use during the guided discussion portion of the lesson. There are also suggested responses to questions to help students grasp the various concepts. These are provided to assist the discussion and are not considered as "right or wrong" responses.

# 1. Summarize the Day/Age theory and the problems associated with it.

The Day/Age theory attempts to merge evolution and creation by stating that each day in Genesis is not a literal 24-hour day but rather a geological age. Each day is said to represent millions of years.

The problems are:

The order of creation in Genesis is different than the geological tables used by evolutionists which have species listed from simple to complex. Creation has complex forms of life appearing at approximately the same time.

The Day/Age theory has death (sin) entering the world before Adam which is the opposite of what scripture explains.

The grammar, context and historical understanding supports a 24-hour period and not the geological age. To state otherwise is to stretch meaning to fit the theory rather than the accepting scripture for what it simply states. Also, note that there is no evidence in scripture to support the Day/Age theory.

## 2. Summarize the activities happening in Genesis 1:3-5.

Light is created. God spoke light into existence. He called light out of darkness. God has not created the sun yet. It will be created later but for this period of creation, the earth is existing through a light and darkness created by God.

The "tri-une" nature of God is revealed. The concept of Tri-une or Trinity means that God is in the form of God the Father (Creator), God the Son (Savior) and God the Holy Spirit (Giver of life and Teacher). God the Father is the source of all things and the Holy Spirit is the energizer. The Word is the revealer of all things (Light). God the Father is the source of our salvation. He sends the Word in the incarnate (God becoming flesh) form of Jesus to reveal and put into motion the plan of salvation. The Holy Spirit energizes the Son (miracles and resurrection) and provides the disciples with spiritual gifts to continue the plan. The Holy Spirit today guides and teaches us as we discover and submit to God's will.

The day and night cycle is established. This is the foundation of life from the beginning. God did His work in light. Life depends on this cycle drawing energy from light. Life has a naturally slower pace in the darkness. Note also that God did not abolish darkness, He only separated it.

### 3. How can you use this lesson to grow spiritually and help others come into a relationship with Jesus?

One can see this as a metaphor of calling us out of darkness into the light of God's love. God created using a methodical and purposeful process to provide a world in which His greatest creation, man, could thrive. This is the environment He wants us to once again live in. He promises to create a new heaven and new earth where He will once again dwell with man (Revelation 21:1-4).

Accepting God's word is the basis of our faith. It is by faith that we accept what we cannot understand and express our trust (Hebrews 11:3). Our faith is what pleases God (Hebrews 11:6).

# Lesson 7 – Day 2 and 3

## Teaching Strategy

The focus of this lesson continues with the creation of our universe by God. Of special note in this lesson are God's activities on day 2 and 3.

## Student Learning Outcomes

- **Know**:  Understand the reality of creation as recorded in Genesis 1.

- **Feel**:  Defend the reality of creation as recorded in Genesis 1.

- **Do**:  Use the information gained from Genesis to strengthen our faith.

## Support

- Series – Genesis – Foundational Book of the Bible (Mike Mazzalongo)

- Video – Lesson 7 – Day 2 and 3

- Student Note Guide for Lesson 7

## Body of the Lesson

1.1    Day 2
1.2    Day 3
1.2    Lessons

# Discussion Questions

Below are suggested questions to use during the guided discussion portion of the lesson. There are also suggested responses to questions to help students grasp the various concepts. These are provided to assist the discussion and are not considered as "right or wrong" responses.

## 1. Summarize the main elements of the Genesis creation account from Genesis 1:1-5.

God created the heavens and earth without form, energy or light. At that point we see the creation of space, time and matter. God's Spirit energized the creation followed by God creating light separating the creation from darkness. This represented the first day of creation.

## 2. Summarize the events of day 2 of the Genesis creation account (Genesis 1:6-8).

During this day God creates the sky. It is described as an expanse or firmament. It is the atmosphere above us. God creates a unique atmosphere that will enable life on earth. It is separated by two bands of water, one above and one below the atmosphere. (verse 7).

**3. How does the world we live in today differ from the world at the time of creation?**

God created our world and universe as the perfect place for man and the rest of His creation to live. It would have everything needed to sustain life. In today's world the perfection of the original creation has been and continues to be degraded.

**4. Summarize the events of day 3 from the Genesis creation account (Genesis 1:9-10) and state the importance of these.**

God brings about land to separate the waters on earth. The water is referred to as seas and the ground as earth. The earth was now ready for the next events of creation, plants, animals and man. It is not stated in the creation account, but the land would be perfect for life to exist containing all the necessary minerals and nutrients. It would not be barren desert since the water from the atmosphere would provide the perfect amount of moisture.

**5. How can you use this lesson to grow spiritually and help others come into a relationship with Jesus?**

God knows and provides what is best for us. His original creation was exactly what was needed for all forms of life, especially man to live with Him. He promises to recreate a world for us so that we will be able to live with Him again (Revelation 21:1-4). However, unless we are in Christ (Romans 6:3-11) we will not experience this blessed reunion.

# Lesson 8 – Day 3 and 4

## Teaching Strategy

The focus of this lesson is the creation of our universe by God.
Of special note in this lesson are the observations of days 3 and 4 of creation.

## Student Learning Outcomes

- **Know**:  Understand the reality of creation as recorded in Genesis 1.

- **Feel**:  Defend the reality of creation as recorded in Genesis 1.

- **Do**:  Use the information gained from Genesis to strengthen our faith.

## Support

- Series – Genesis – Foundational Book of the Bible (Mike Mazzalongo)

- Video – Lesson 8 – Day 3 and 4

- Student Note Guide for Lesson 8

## Body of the Lesson

1.1    Day 3
1.2    Day 4
1.3    Lessons

# Discussion Questions

Below are suggested questions to use during the guided discussion portion of the lesson.
There are also suggested responses to questions to help students grasp the various concepts.
These are provided to assist the discussion and are not considered as "right or wrong"
responses.

**1. Summarize the events that occurred on day 3 of creation from Genesis 1:9-13. What stands out about these?**

God creates land and separates the water on earth calling them seas. He also creates vegetation as well as the cycle of life for vegetation (fruit and seeds).

Answers will vary regarding what stands out. Some key points of interest include: God's orderly and purposeful process, not only did God create the elements but He put into place the process so life could continue. Note also that God "saw that it was good." This is not just a statement of finality, it is also a statement of quality. God's creation was not a process that took eons of time. It happened in one motion and was what God intended.

**2. Summarize the events that occurred on day 4 of creation from Genesis 1:14-19. What stands out about these?**

God creates the sun, moon and stars. He also sets the seasons.

Answers will vary regarding what stands out. Some key points of interest include: God continues the cycle of life expanded to seasons, days and years. The seasons would have been different than what we experience due to the steady environment provided by the perfect condition and function of water and earth at that time. What we know as the four seasons would come later, after Adam and Eve were driven from Eden. The seasons as we know them symbolize the life cycle of birth, growth and death. Also note that God created a mature universe, earth and environment. Light was created along with the source of light.

**3. What is the difference between the light given by the sun and the light given by the moon?**

The sun is a source of light whereas the moon reflects the light of the sun. The moon does not generate light itself.

**4. Summarize the first four days of creation in your own words.**

The intent of this question is for students to comprehend the orderliness of God's creative activities. We can see from this that God has a plan and creates in such a way that each part of creation enables the next part to appear with proper support.

Day 1 - Time, space, matter, light and dark cycle
Day 2 - Water, atmosphere, water canopy
Day 3 - Water and land separated, vegetation
Day 4 – Sun, moon and stars

## 5. How can you use this lesson to grow spiritually and help others come into a relationship with Jesus?

God created a perfect world for man. Man allowed sin to enter the creation and destroy the perfect relationship he had with God. God seeks to reestablish the relationship through Jesus. The process of reconciliation is in place, but we have to make the move to respond to God's grace. We do so when we recognize Jesus as our Lord, repent (turn to Jesus) and submit to baptism (Acts 2:38). This does not re-establish our physical environment but does re-establish our spiritual relationship.

# Lesson 9 – Day 5 and 6

## Teaching Strategy

The focus of this lesson is the creation of our universe by God.
Of special note are the activities and the importance of these on day 5 and 6 of creation.

## Student Learning Outcomes

- Know:  Understand the reality of creation as recorded in Genesis 1.

- Feel:  Defend the reality of creation as recorded in Genesis 1.

- Do:  Use the information gained from Genesis to strengthen our faith.

## Support

- Series – Genesis – Foundational Book of the Bible (Mike Mazzalongo)

- Video – Lesson 9 – Day 5 and 6

- Student Note Guide for Lesson 9

## Body of the Lesson

1.1     Day 5
1.2     Day 6
1.3     Lessons

# Discussion Questions

Below are suggested questions to use during the guided discussion portion of the lesson. There are also suggested responses to questions to help students grasp the various concepts. These are provided to assist the discussion and are not considered as "right or wrong" responses.

**1. Summarize the creation events that occurred on day 5 of creation from Genesis 1:20-23 and what stands out to you about the process?**

On the fifth day of creation God created the life that exists in water as well as the birds of the air. This represents the creation of a higher form of life than plants. He also created the continuation of life according of its own kind. God blessed them and gave the qualifier that this activity was good. Note also that Genesis records this in a day using the specific language of morning and evening. This supports the measurement we know as time. It also supports that the life in the water and air were created as mature life fully capable of reproduction. The ability to reproduce is an indicator of this life.

This demonstrates that God had a methodical plan rather than random actions with no purpose.

**2. What is the difference between the order of evolution model of life and that which is recorded in Genesis?**

- Evolution – Marine organisms – land plants – Birds
- Genesis – Land plants – Marine organisms – Birds

The evolutionist says that the system of life goes from smallest to greatest. Genesis records that the largest marine creatures were made first.

**3. Summarize the events that occurred on day 6 of creation as recorded in Genesis 1:24-25. What stands out about the process?**

God creates life on earth in the form of cattle, creeping things and beasts according to their kind. Just as with the creation of life in the seas and air, this represents a continuation of the creation of higher forms of life. These were categorized differently than the forms of life in the seas and air. Furthermore, these creatures were created as mature animals with the ability to reproduce and continue their forms of life.

Yet again, God is showing organization and purpose in His activities. He creates the environment to support increasingly higher forms of life.

**4. How can you use this lesson to grow spiritually and help others come into a relationship with Jesus?**

Just as with the other days of creations, God offers us a simple explanation of His creation in Genesis 1. Man tries to complicate or explain it away to weaken our faith which is one of the strategies Satan uses to separate us from God. We must simply accept God's word as truth, even if we don't fully understand it. God will grant us understanding as He wills. If we do not accept God's account of creation, then we undermine the truthfulness of all other scripture, especially His promise to reconcile us to Him through Jesus.

# Lesson 10 – The Creation of Man

## Teaching Strategy

The focus of this lesson is on God's creation of man and the significance of this action. Of special note in this lesson is an explanation of what it means for man to be made in the image of God and God's reason for creating man.

## Student Learning Outcomes

- Know:  Understand how Genesis builds faith as an inspired work of God.

- Feel:  Develop an awareness for the role that Genesis plays in God's overall plan for man.

- Do:  Use the information gained from Genesis to strengthen our faith.

## Support

- Series – Genesis – Foundational Book of the Bible (Mike Mazzalongo)

- Video – Lesson 10 – The Creation of Man

- Student Note Guide for Lesson 10

## Body of the Lesson

1.1    The divine council
1.2    God's charge to man
1.3    Lessons

# Discussion Questions

Below are suggested questions to use during the guided discussion portion of the lesson. There are also suggested responses to questions to help students grasp the various concepts. These are provided to assist the discussion and are not considered as "right or wrong" responses.

**1. Summarize the actions of creation up to the point of God's creation of man and how these actions support one another.**

The intent of this question is to reinforce how God had an organized process and purpose in creation.

God created the inanimate world: matter, atmosphere, vegetation.
These possessed no consciousness on their part. They were the foundation of life yet to be created. God then created the animate world: fish, birds, and animals. This represented consciousness but were not in the full image of God as man would be.

All these activities were done in an orderly and purposeful manner to support the next act of creation. The creation of time, space and matter enabled the earth and all of its elements to be created and sustained. Then plant life and animal life were created with the necessary environment to sustain them as well.

**2. In what ways are the inanimate elements and the animate elements of creation alike? How are they different?**

They share a common creator, are interdependent and supportive, and can reproduce. They differ in their level of consciousness, self-awareness and level of spiritual awareness.

### 3. What is significant about God's statement in Genesis 1:26a?

Responses will vary but if not stated, include: This is the first indication of God's dynamic nature with the use of the plural pronoun "Us" in reference to Himself. This also states that God is endowing elements of His own character and being in His creation of man. He did not impart these to the other parts of creation.

### 4. What is meant by man created in the image of God?

"Image" has many related concepts, for example: resemblance, figure, model or shape. Put together we see that man is made to resemble God. This does not mean that man possesses all the characteristics or qualities of God. Later, Satan would use this reality as part of his plan to bring sin into the world as he interacts with Eve (Genesis 3:5). However, there are characteristics man possesses that are gifts from God such as free will, the ability to communicate and other qualities beyond the capabilities of creatures brought forth earlier.

### 5. How does man possess the nature of God?

Man is formed from inanimate elements (matter). He has consciousness like animate creatures and is also aware of himself. Man possesses the spiritual nature of God which includes free will, the ability to communicate with all of creation, including other humans and God Himself.

Although animals communicate, it is in a much more limited way. Other elements creation elements lack the qualities of free will and a sense of morality. Other creatures react from instinct rather than reason and purpose as does man. Furthermore, man's spiritual nature is eternal.

## 6. What is man's position in relation to the rest of creation (Genesis 1:26b)?

God placed man over creation. God's use of the term "dominion" means man is to reign over or be over creation. This is more of a stewardship role where man interacts with creation for its continued existence and purpose.

## 7. Summarize God's charge to man in Genesis 1:28-31 and what is meant by the expression "very good"?

God commissions man to thrive in the environment He created for him. God indicates that everything He created is to sustain and enable man to live. This is summed up with the statement that "it was very good." This added emphasis shows God's satisfaction with His creation. All of creation, including man, has not been created in a pure and sinless environment.

## 8. How can you use this lesson to grow spiritually and help others come into a relationship with Jesus?

Man was not an afterthought of God. God clearly creates a perfect environment to sustain life for His greatest and crowning achievement, the creation of man. Man was in the image of God, including the ability to choose. Sadly, we do not always choose wisely. For that reason, God also created a plan through which we can be reconciled to Him. This plan is fulfilled through His Son, Jesus. Jesus is the only way to be reconciled to God (John 14:6). We must believe this and act upon it as God directs and help others come to this knowledge as well.

# Lesson 11 – God's Rest and Man's Creation

## Teaching Strategy

The focus of this lesson is on the completion of God's creative actions in the creation of man. Of special note in this lesson is the concept of rest and God's intimate actions in the creation of man.

## Student Learning Outcomes

- **Know**: Understand how Genesis builds faith as an inspired work of God.

- **Feel**: Develop an awareness of the role Genesis plays in God's overall plan for man.

- **Do**: Use the information gained from Genesis to strengthen faith.

## Support

- Series – Genesis – Foundation Book of the Bible (Mike Mazzalongo)

- Video – Lesson 11 – God's Rest and Man's Creation

- Student Note Guide for Lesson 11

## Body of the Lesson

1.1     The day of rest
1.2     Generational division of Genesis
1.2.1   Adam's perspective
1.2.2   Pre-sin environment
1.2.3   The creation of man
1.3     Lessons

# Discussion Questions

Below are suggested questions to use during the guided discussion portion of the lesson. There are also suggested responses to questions to help students grasp the various concepts. These are provided to assist the discussion and are not considered as "right or wrong" responses.

### 1. What are some implications of the word, "rested" as used in Genesis 2:1-3?

The use of the word rested in this passage signifies completion of actions and to refrain from further actions related to creation. God completed His creative work as He planned. The object of His creation was to prepare an environment for man to live and thrive. Once this was completed, God refrained from further creative acts. All was completed.

### 2. What action did God do regarding the seventh day and what was a related activity for Israel?

God sanctified the seventh day meaning He set it aside as special and sacred. Later, in Exodus 20:8, He commands Israel to set aside the sabbath as a day of rest. They were to use that day, not only to refrain from labor, but to also meditate on God and all He had done for Israel.

### 3. What is the relationship between Genesis 1:1 and Genesis 2:4?

Genesis 1:1 is the introduction to God's creative acts. Genesis 2:4 serves as a transitional summary laying the foundation for details concerning the creation of man. **Note**: The expression, "in the day" does not mean all were created in one day. Rather it is used as a general time period. Some use a similar expression, "In the day" or "In my day". Genesis 1 continues to give the details of the six days of creation.

## 4. How does Genesis 2:5-6 describe the earth before man was created and what does this signify?

Before man was created there was no vegetation or rain. A mist and subterranean rivers provided water. It serves as a transition from pre-man and sin to God's creation of man. It is a wide-angle view rather than a detailed view.

## 5. Summarize how God created man from Genesis 2:7 and answer the following questions.

God formed man from the earth and breathed life into him.

### How was man formed (Genesis 1:26)?

Man was made in the image of God. Although matter from which man was made was of the earth, the likeness of God (God's nature, character, spiritual elements, etc) were from God.

**What is different between breathing life into man and the creation of animals?**

Animals were created already conscious, but man was brought into consciousness by God's breath. God spoke animals into creation, but we see a special action with man. God "forms" man then by breathing life into Him, He imparts His own self into man. This shows the intimate relationship and special position of man. **Note**: Animals were not created in the image of God, only man was created in this way. Therefore, the evolutionist's view of man evolving form lower forms of life is not possible. Animals do not possess the same spiritual and moral characteristics as man.

## 6. How can you use this lesson to grow spiritually and help others come into a relationship with Jesus?

This detail of man's creation shows the love that God has for man. Man's sin (rebellion) against God destroyed that special relationship. He set in motion a way for the relationship to be restored through Jesus. John 1:1-3 states that Jesus (The Word) was involved in the creation events. In God's plan to redeem man we see that through Jesus, man once again receives life (Romans 6:3-5).

# Lesson 12 – The Moral Choice

## Teaching Strategy

The focus of this lesson is to understand the physical and moral environment of man. Of special note in this lesson is how God placed man in a special environment and allowed him the ability to choose. This shows how God created in man a spiritual nature and gave him the freedom to exercise it.

## Student Learning Outcomes

- **Know**: Understand how Genesis builds faith as an inspired work of God.

- **Feel**: Develop an awareness of the role Genesis plays in God's overall plan for man.

- **Do**: Use the information gained from Genesis to strengthen our faith.

## Support

- Series – Genesis – Foundational Book of the Bible (Mike Mazzalongo)

- Video – Lesson 12 – The Moral Choice

- Student Note Guide for Lesson 12

## Body of the Lesson

1.1    The garden
1.2    The moral choice
1.3    Lessons

# Discussion Questions

Below are suggested questions to use during the guided discussion portion of the lesson. There are also suggested responses to questions to help students grasp the various concepts. These are provided to assist the discussion and are not considered as "right or wrong" responses.

# 1. Summarize the events of Genesis 2:8-14 and answer the following questions.

God has now completed creating an environment for man and has brought him to life. He now prepares a special place for Adam to live.

**What is significant about the Garden?**

It had everything needed to sustain life for man. It was not simply a basic life but a place that provided a perfect quality of physical life on earth.

**What two specific trees were placed in the garden and what were their significance?**

The tree of life symbolized spiritual truth or a source of life sustaining properties. This reinforces the view that God created man as an eternal being. God did not forbid man from eating of this tree.

The tree of knowledge of good and evil represents the results or consequences of choice. It was a physical used to exercise man's free will.

**Why are the geographical properties described in Genesis 2:10-14 not present today?**

The flood changed the topography of the world. Furthermore, when God banished man from the garden, He removed the possibility then and now of its discovery. It no longer exists in the form of its original creation.

## 2. Why did God place man in the garden and what is the implication for us today (Genesis 2:15)?

God placed man in the garden to cultivate it and keep it in order to provide for his needs. This reveals one of the reasons for man's creation, which was to serve. Adam not only enjoyed the benefits of his relationship with God and the management of the garden, he also benefited by having a sense of purpose. Obeying and serving God as well as serving others gives one a complete and satisfying sense of purpose and meaning in life.

## 3. Why did God give man a choice rather than simply creating a being without free will?

God created man as a physical creature with a spiritual nature. Man connects with God on a spiritual level. The spiritual level is expressed through man's moral nature. The foundation of the moral nature is the ability to choose. **Note**: We see this in our lives today as we interact with each other. We are physically connected as fellow humans but spiritually connected by love and friendship which are emotions largely based on choice.

## 4. Why did God bring every creature before Adam to name?

This demonstrated Adam's dominion over the creation. It also showed Adam that there was no suitable companion for him. It awakened him to a need for companionship with his own kind. It further showed another characteristic of being created in the image of God; our intelligence. God not only allowed us choice but allows us intelligence to reason and make good choices. Our challenge is to choose according to God's will.

**Other items of note**:
- Adam was created with intelligence and the ability to communicate
- Adam recognized the role of animals
- Adam was created superior to the animals.

## 5. What is the significance of Eve being created from Adam rather than the earth as Adam was?

This creates a unique relationship between them. They are not two separate creations as much as interrelated creations. Eve represents a completing process. God recognized the value of companionship. Perhaps this was also indicative of the special nature of God. We see God as a triune God with a dynamic and pluralistic inner nature. Thus, the statement that it is not good for man to be alone suggests that in marriage, man and woman most resemble God's complex being.

## 6. How can you use this lesson to grow spiritually and help others come into a relationship with Jesus?

From the details of Adam's creation, the garden and Adam's role, we see God's love and desire for a special relationship with His creation. It was God's intent that this relationship be close and purposeful. Jesus was there at our original creation and is now a part of our recreated spiritual life (Romans 6:1-11). Just as with Adam, we make the choice in reestablishing this relationship. We must use our intelligence, therefore, to choose wisely.

# Lesson 13 – The Creation of Woman

## Teaching Strategy

The focus of this lesson is to review the final actions God took to complete His creation. Of special note in this lesson is the significance of creating a suitable companion for Adam.

## Student Learning Outcomes

- **Know**: Understand how Genesis demonstrates the love God has for His creation.

- **Feel**: Develop an awareness of the role Genesis plays in God's overall plan for man.

- **Do**: Use the information gained from Genesis to strengthen our faith.

## Support

- Series – Genesis – Foundational Book of the Bible (Mike Mazzalongo)

- Video – Lesson 13 – The Creation of Woman

- Student Note Guide for Lesson 13

## Body of the Lesson

1.1     Process of creating woman
1.2     The significance of creating woman
1.3     Lessons

# Discussion Questions

Below are suggested questions to use during the guided discussion portion of the lesson. There are also suggested responses to questions to help students grasp the various concepts. These are provided to assist the discussion and are not considered as "right or wrong" responses.

# 1. Summarize how God created woman and discuss its significance.

After stating that man should not be alone and no suitable companion was currently found for him in what had so far been created, God caused Adam to sleep. He then took a portion of Adam's side and formed woman.

Answers will vary regarding the significance of this action. Some suggestions:

- Woman is part of man. They are interconnected and interdependent to create and sustain further human life.
- The two are compatible with each other.
- Selecting from Adam's side symbolizes that they serve side by side.
- She is to be a helpmeet; helping Adam meet his need and purpose in serving God.
- Her characteristics and nature were human but her likeness, like Adam's, was in the image of God.

# 2. What did Adam call this new creation and what was the significance of this?

Adam named her woman because she was taken from man. Adam acknowledged both her differences and her compatibility to himself.

# 3. What is the significance of Genesis 2:24?

It states the formation of the family as God intended. It further establishes the process whereby new families will be formed as independently functioning units. This new family does not diminish God's family plan but enhances it and guarantees the continuation of His creation.

## 4. Defend the statement that the family serves as the foundation of society.

Answers will vary. The intent of this question is to explore God's will in contrast with man's will. It will also serve as a basis for discussion in later lessons when students will examine the consequences when man disregards God's will.

Clearly God's intent is one woman for one man. God gave no indication for any other form of family. If the family fails, then society has no foundation for sustained growth, moral integrity and the continued search for God's will.

## 5. Explain how the three elements of intimacy, exclusivity and longevity provide for the success of a marriage.

**Intimacy** – This describes the closeness between a couple not available in other relationships. This nourishes the trust and commitment that a marriage needs to succeed.

**Exclusivity** – This involves the absolute focus on each other physically, socially and on a spiritual level.

**Longevity** – God did not place a timeline on the relationship. Since death had not yet entered into man's existence the implication is that the marriage is for life. To this end, New Testament verses teach that only death or marital infidelity form the basis for dissolving the marriage.

Elements of these three may be present in a relationship but the more each of these are involved in an appropriately balanced way, the stronger the marriage remains as God intended.

## 6. How can you use this lesson to grow spiritually and help others come into a relationship with Jesus?

God clearly has, as part of His purpose for man, that all his need be met. By creating a suitable companion in the form of a woman, God provided what Adam needed for his physical, social and spiritual needs. God continues to provide for our greatest need through His Son, Jesus. Through Jesus our need for forgiveness of sin and reconciliation to God is provided. Woman was created from and for man.

God came to earth in the form of the man, Jesus Christ. He came forth from the woman God created to fulfill the role of Savior of all man and women.

# Lesson 14 –
# The First Appearance of Satan in the Bible

## Teaching Strategy

The focus of this lesson is to see how Satan brought sin into the world.
Of special note in this lesson is how scripture describes Satan.

## Student Learning Outcomes

- **Know**:  Understand how sin separated God from man.

- **Feel**:  Develop an awareness of the role Genesis plays in God's overall plan for man.

- **Do**:  Use the information gained from Genesis to strengthen our faith.

## Support

- Series – Genesis – Foundational Book of the Bible (Mike Mazzalongo)

- Video – Lesson 14 – The First Appearance of Satan in the Bible

- Student Note Guide for Lesson 14

## Body of the Lesson

1.1    Satan
1.2    Satan and the Serpent
1.3    Lessons

# Discussion Questions

Below are suggested questions to use during the guided discussion portion of the lesson.
There are also suggested responses to questions to help students grasp the various concepts.
These are provided to assist the discussion and are not considered as "right or wrong"
responses.

**1. How does Genesis 3:1 describe Satan (the serpent – Revelation 12:9) and how to you understand the word used?**

The intent of this question is to help clarify how Genesis describes Satan. Later this will be more important as we see the actions Satan uses to bring sin into the world.

Different versions use different words, but the most common description is, "More crafty than any beast of the field." The word "crafty" is generally used in a negative way. Certainly, as the passage continues, we see it as a negative description.

**2. What similarities are there between the descriptions of Satan from Genesis 3:1, Isaiah 14:12-15, Ezekiel 28:12-19, and 1 Peter 5:8?**

Answers will vary. Look for such things as: Satan is cunning, prideful, powerful and ruthless. His intent is to destroy the relationship between God and man. He knows he cannot attack God directly, so he attempts to destroy God's greatest creation, man.

### 3. How does Paul in Romans 5:12 describe the entrance of sin into creation?

Sin did not exist in creation until Satan seduced Eve into disobedience. It was through Adam's poor use of the gifts of intelligence and choice that Satan was able to separate man from God.

**4. How can you use this lesson to grow spiritually and help others come into a relationship with Jesus?**

Although Satan brought sin into creation, we must understand that man had a role in the fall. Even though man was separated from God because of sin, God reconciled him through Jesus Christ. It is only through Christ that we can return to God (John 14:6). We must accept the responsibility for sin in our lives and return to Him. God's grace provided a sacrifice for our sin through Jesus and our faith in Him enables our reconciliation with God.

# Lesson 15 – Eve's 5 Mistakes

## Teaching Strategy

The focus of this lesson is to review the first sin.  Of special note in this lesson is how Satan tempted Eve and the mistakes she made that resulted in her disobedience and subsequent fall.

## Student Learning Outcomes

- **Know**:  Understand how sin separates God from man.

- **Feel**:  Develop an awareness of the role Genesis plays in God's overall plan for man.

- **Do**:  Use the information gained from Genesis to strengthen our faith.

## Support

- Series – Genesis – Foundational Book of the Bible (Mike Mazzalongo)

- Video – Lesson 15 – Eve's 5 Mistakes

- Student Note Guide for Lesson 15

## Body of the Lesson

1.1     Summary of the first Sin
1.2     Eve's mistakes
1.2     Lessons

# Discussion Questions

Below are suggested questions to use during the guided discussion portion of the lesson. There are also suggested responses to questions to help students grasp the various concepts. These are provided to assist the discussion and are not considered as "right or wrong" responses.

## 1. Summarize Genesis 3:1-6.

Answers will vary but in short, Satan, in the form of a serpent tempted Eve to eat fruit from the Tree of Knowledge of Good and Evil which had been forbidden by God.

## 2. What was the basic sin committed by Adam and Eve and what was the motivation behind it?

The basic sin was direct disobedience to God's prohibition of eating of the tree of knowledge of good and evil. The motivation behind it seems to be a combination of doubt and pride. Satan injected doubt by his statement in verse 4. An appeal to her pride (that Eve could be like God) is behind Satan's promise in verse 5.

## 3. What is the difference between the statement in Genesis 1:26, "Let us make man in our image, after our likeness." and Satan's statement in Genesis 3:5, "you will be like God..."?

Genesis 1:26 is a declaration of God's will. Genesis 3:5 is simply a questioning of this statement. Eve was already like God. One of the elements of being made in God's image was the ability to choose. Satan twisted that characteristic to use it against God.

## 4. Compare the temptation of Adam and Eve with the temptation of Jesus from Matthew 5 and answer the following questions.

### What are some similarities between the two events?

In Matthew 5 Satan uses the tactic of doubt with his statement in the first two temptations, "If you are the Son of God…".   It can be argued that Satan also tried to appeal to pride by demanding Jesus demonstrate His power (turning stones to bread and throwing himself down from the tower).  Satan also tried to have Jesus lower His faith/trust in God (prove He will save Him).  The final temptation of offering Jesus Kingship if he would worship Satan was an attempt at rulership without the price of the cross.

### What did Jesus ultimately do to defeat Satan's attacks that Adam and Eve did not do?

Jesus commanded Satan to be gone (Matthew 5:10).
Adam and Eve did not dismiss Satan, but continued to interact with him.

## 5. Summarize each of the 5 mistakes Eve made in response to Satan's temptations.

- She compromised with a rebel
- She changed God's word
- She considered the offer
- She disobeyed
- She led Adam to sin

## 6. How can you use this lesson to grow spiritually and help others come into a relationship with Jesus?

We must realize that God has our best interests at heart because He created us and knows our needs. Yet, in His love for us, He gives us the choice to obey Him. His command to Adam and Eve was simple: do not eat. Today, we have the same choice to obey or not to obey God's commands. We demonstrate that obedience through our faithful submission to the gospel by believing in Jesus and expressing our faith through repentance and baptism (Acts 2:38). Just as Satan attacked Adam and Eve, he attacks us with similar tactics of doubt (i.e. baptism is not necessary for salvation) and pride ("I'm OK...I don't need God" or "I'll obey God on my terms").

# Lesson 16 – The Judgment

### Teaching Strategy

The focus of this lesson is to review the immediate consequences of sin. Of special note in this lesson is the pattern of sin and the judgment that resulted from the original sin.

### Student Learning Outcomes

- **Know**: Explain how God demonstrates His love for man during the judgment for their sin.

- **Feel**: Develop an appreciation for the love that God has for us.

- **Do**: Resolve to live faithfully in response to God's love.

### Support

- Series – Genesis – Foundational Book of the Bible (Mike Mazzalongo)

- Video – Lesson 16 – The Judgment

- Student Note Guide for Lesson 16

### Body of the Lesson

1.1    The pattern of sin
1.2    The resulting judgment
1.3    Lessons

## Discussion Questions

Below are suggested questions to use during the guided discussion portion of the lesson. There are also suggested responses to questions to help students grasp the various concepts. These are provided to assist the discussion and are not considered as "right or wrong" responses.

**1. From the text provided for this lesson, summarize the pattern for most sin and how this compares to James 1:14-15.**

The general pattern is that we fail to rebuke (challenge) sin when the temptation appears. We find ourselves compromising God's word. We then consider the short-term pleasure from the sin and eventually consent to the sinful action.

James 1:14-15 provides a similar pattern. He states that we are not tempted by God, but by our own desires. This desire, if not checked results in sin, which, as in the case of Adam and Eve, leads to death.

**2. Summarize the sequence of events following sin from Genesis 3:6-13 and the results from their sin.**

Eve gave in to the temptation to eat from the tree of knowledge of good and evil. Adam also ate of the fruit. They felt the shame of what they had done and lost their innocence. When God appeared in the garden, they hid from Him. When confronted, Adam blamed Eve for giving him the fruit to eat. Eve blamed Satan for deceiving her.

Their action resulted in shame from knowingly disobeying God; acknowledgement of guilt following their sin, fearfulness to face God, more sin by Adam in blaming Eve, and Eve blaming Satan, rather than admitting their failure.

## 3. What was the judgment brought on those who were involved in the original sin?

Satan was cursed into an eternally low position in creation, Eve was placed into submission to Adam and experience pain in childbirth, and Adam was cursed with ongoing struggle to draw his needs from the earth. Ultimately both Adam and Eve would experience physical death and return to the dust of the earth from which God formed them.

## 4. How can you use this lesson to grow spiritually and help others come into a relationship with Jesus?

In Genesis 3:15, among the statements of judgment for sin, God presents the first indication of His plan for man to be reconciled to Him. It would eventually play out in the death of Jesus as a sacrifice for our sins.

In Romans 5, Paul states that just as sin entered the world through one man, through another man (Jesus) salvation would be provided to all men.

God does not demand that we be sinless before expressing His love for us. While we are in our sins, He offers us forgiveness and reconciliation so we can experience the peace and joy of renewal through Christ here on earth, and the hope of resurrection and eternal life after we die (Romans 6:4-10).

# Lesson 17 – Paradise Lost

## Teaching Strategy

The focus of this lesson is to review the consequences of sin on man's relationship with God. Of special note in this lesson is the consequences experienced by Adam and Eve and the creation following God's judgment.

## Student Learning Outcomes

- **Know**: Explain how sin destroys our relationship with God.

- **Feel**: Develop an appreciation for the love that God has for us.

- **Do**: Resolve to live faithfully in response to God's love.

## Support

- Series – Genesis – Foundational Book of the Bible (Mike Mazzalongo)

- Video – Lesson 17 – Paradise Lost

- Student Note Guide for Lesson 17

## Body of the Lesson

1.1    The judgment of man
1.2    Paradise lost
1.3    Lessons

# Discussion Questions

Below are suggested questions to use during the guided discussion portion of the lesson. There are also suggested responses to questions to help students grasp the various concepts. These are provided to assist the discussion and are not considered as "right or wrong" responses.

## 1. Summarize God's judgment on Adam from Genesis 3:17-19.

God identifies the sin Adam committed. He then brings judgment against Adam because he disobeyed the command to not eat from the tree of knowledge of good and evil. Because they did so, God now requires struggle to maintain their existence. He also fulfills the consequence of death as a result of this disobedience. It would not be an immediate physical death, but it would happen gradually.

## 2. Read James 4:7 and 1 Corinthians 10:13. What do these verses teach about temptation and how does this relate to the sin of Adam and Eve?

James 4:7 states that if we resist Satan then he will flee from us. 1 Corinthians 10:13 promises that God will not allow us to be tempted beyond our ability to resist.

God allowed Adam and Eve to be tempted. They had the ultimate responsibility for their actions. Both could have refused the temptation. They clearly knew God's prohibition of eating from the tree. Furthermore, Adam could have refused Eve's offer of the fruit. This is true for us today. We are ultimately responsible before God for our sins. No matter the temptation, it is our responsibility to resist sin.

## 3. Describe the impact on creation before and after sin.

Before sin, the world was a perfect environment for man. There was no death, hardship from the environment, disease or other ills that face man today. The earth provided everything needed to sustain life. After sin, the elements to sustain life were still present but degraded and now struggle would be required to sustain life. Before sin, God declared that His creation was "very good." After sin, the creation would suffer the same downward cycle of life and death that man would now experience. Not only would the earth not easily provide elements needed for life, the environment now would be hostile to man's existence. The ultimate hardship was physical and spiritual separation from God. This would be seen in spiritual alienation and physical death.

## 4. What are some of the consequences both man the creation would suffer because of sin?

Sorrow, continual disappointment, futility in life, pain, suffering, hard work and death.

## 5. What was the significance of renaming Eve?

Prior to sin, Eve was known simply as, "woman" showing her equal standing with Adam. Following sin, she is renamed as Eve, meaning "life-giver." Furthermore, she would be subject to Adam, her husband, in order to avoid the chaos in the family that would naturally arise because of sin.

Her name showed her role as the vehicle by which life would continue in the world. God stated in His judgment on Eve that she would suffer in childbearing, however, she would be blessed by the ultimate birth of Jesus as the Savior of mankind (the "seed" would ultimately come from her womb).

## 6. What did God do to cover Adam and Eve's shame for their sin and what was its significance?

Their shame was immediately seen in their realization of their nakedness. God provided animal skins as a covering for them. The significance of this is that it was the first sacrifice made on behalf of man. The animals involved with this sacrifice were sinless. In like manner, Jesus would be offered as a sinless sacrifice to cover the shame for our sins.

## 7. What action did God take to protect Adam and Eve after He pronounced judgement on them (Genesis 3:22-24)?

God recognized that Adam and Eve could eat of the tree of life and thus live forever in a sinful state. He removed them from the Garden to protect them from this terrible consequence. He then placed a guard so they could not reenter the Garden.

## 8. How can you use this lesson to grow spiritually and help others come into a relationship with Jesus?

As stated in the associated text, "God placed a curse on the earth by withdrawing Himself and thus allowing the world and man to disintegrate into death. However, He did not leave the world without hope. That hope was that one day He would create a new heaven and a new earth which would never be destroyed by sin and where He would dwell eternally with His people."

We can regain access to paradise and the tree of life only through Jesus Christ. This is the promise from Revelation 2:7. This promise is to everyone who believes and obeys the gospel.

# Lesson 18 – Cain and Abel

## Teaching Strategy

The focus of this lesson are the events leading to the first murder. Of special note in this lesson is how this sin continued the path of the fall of the world originally begun by Adam and Eve.

## Student Learning Outcomes

- **Know**: Understand the impact of sin.
- **Feel**: Resolve to combat sin.
- **Do**: Use the lessons from Genesis to grow spiritually.

## Support

- Series – Genesis – Foundational Book of the Bible (Mike Mazzalongo)
- Video – Lesson 18 – Cain and Abel
- Student Note Guide for Lesson 18

## Body of the Lesson

1.1     The Murder of Abel
1.2     Dealing with sin
1.3     Lessons

# Discussion Questions

Below are suggested questions to use during the guided discussion portion of the lesson. There are also suggested responses to questions to help students grasp the various concepts. These are provided to assist the discussion and are not considered as "right or wrong" responses.

## 1. Summarize the events of Genesis 4:1-8.

Adam and Eve have two sons, Cain and Abel. Cain becomes angry because God accepts Abel's offering but rejects his offering. He acts upon his anger by murdering his brother, Abel. As a result, Cain is banished from the family, and the presence of the Lord.

## 2. Describe how the punishment of Cain relates to the fact that God's plan of redemption continues even when we, through our sin, work against it and the implication for us.

The intent of this question is for us to understand that although we sin, God allows us to return to Him and continue as faithful servants.

God gave the first indication of His plan for man's redemption in Genesis 3:15. Satan tries to limit God's plan by continuily seeking to destroy the relationship we have with God. God does not change His plan, but He does from time to time redirect us. In the case of Cain and Abel, God removed Cain from the plan and continued it through other children born later to Adam and Eve.

There are many examples of how God uses a person after they've repented and redirects their way. An example of this is King David after he repented from his sin with Bathsheba (2 Samuel 11). God reinstated David as king after his repentance, but the consequences of David's sin remained. God recognized his sincere repentance, but the child conceived by Bathsheba dies. David's other offspring would suffer many problems as well. Yet, God kept His promise to bring the Messiah through David's descendants.

Today, God's plan (will) is that all be saved (1 Timothy 2:1-4). When we as Christians sin and rebel against God, we suffer the consequences. As 1 John 1:7-9 explains, if we are trying to live faithfully and repent of our sin, God continues to forgive and wash us in the blood of Christ. Our salvation is not lost, however, if we do not repent or refuse to acknowledge our sins, then we are at risk of losing our salvation.

### 3. What are some reasons Cain sinned and the implication for us?

The intent of this question is to show that we share in the same reasons for sin as Cain.

Possible reasons for Cain's sin are jealousy, anger and resentment.
God asks Cain for the reason for his anger (Genesis 4:7).

The implication for us is that we also experience the same reasons for sin today. We also are subject to the consequence of sin which is spiritual death unless we repent and strive to live faithfully.

**4. Read Genesis 4:6-7, Ephesians 4:26-27, and Matthew 5:22 and answer the following questions.**

**What is the danger of harboring anger?**

If we do not deal with anger we allow it to destroy our relationship with others. With Cain, anger and resentment eventually destroyed the relationship with his family. Paul warns that it can destroy our relationship with others if we allow anger to continue unchecked.

**What are some potential actions we cannot take if we harbor anger?**

We cannot maintain an effective relationship with the one with whom we are angry. We cannot show the love of God while angry. We cannot teach someone about Jesus while in this state. Anger displaces the love God commands us to have for others.

**Describe situations where anger is appropriate.**

Our Lord demonstrated anger when he cleansed the Temple in Matthew 21:12-13. We can be angry at an unrighteous situation or event and with those involved, however, we should work to resolve the cause of the sin involved. Paul teaches in Ephesians 4:26-27, that we do become angry at times, but says we should try work through the anger as quickly as possible.

## 5. Discuss the following statements on how to deal with sin.

- **Face the problem.** Don't let the emotion resulting in sin continue. Find out why you feel the emotion and formulate a plan to deal with it.

- **Acknowledge your fault.** We must recognize the real reason we've sinned. Perhaps it's a lack of faith. Perhaps it's because of our sinful desires. Whatever the reason, we must not make excuses but recognize the problem and our role in it.

- **Deal with the sin and do not ignore it.** In doing so we have not repented and have the potential of losing our salvation. We must work to control our lives rather than have our lives controlled by the sin. This involves having a plan to prevent sin and to deal with it when it occurs.

## 6. Summarize what Jesus teaches us about dealing with offenses between fellow believers from Matthew 18:15-17.

Jesus teaches us to go to the one involved in a private way to discuss the situation. If that fails, then we are to try again but to have others with us as a witness of our attempt to resolve the situation. If that fails, we then can bring it before the church for resolution. If that fails we must recognize the person as an outsider of our community of believers. This means that our relationship with this person has now changed. We must reteach this person in order to bring them back to repentance so we can bring him or her back into the community of believers. The intent is to maintain unity and to save the soul of the one lost. A note of warning here. We must be very careful that we harbor love in our heart and not hate. If we do not harbor love in our hearts then we are in danger of sin as well.

## 7. How can you use this lesson to grow spiritually and help others come into a relationship with Jesus?

God recognizes our weaknesses. He makes a way for us to return to Him and remain faithful. The initial reconciliation occurs following our conversion by confessing Jesus as our Lord, resolving to live as Jesus teaches us and submitting to baptism. After that, we do continue to sin, however, we do not have to be "rebaptized" each time to receive forgiveness. Rather, we go to God in prayer asking for forgiveness and the blood of Jesus continues to wash us clean (1 John 1:7-9). Praise God that He promises to forgive us when we repent thus continuing to demonstrate His love for us. In doing so, God demonstrates for us that Satan cannot win unless we reject our Lord's invitation to come to Him or to return to Him.

# Lesson 19 – The Punishment of Cain

## Teaching Strategy

The focus of this lesson is on the result of Cain's sin and the punishment meted out to him by God. Of special note in this lesson is the judgment of God, the impact of sin on the family and society through to this day.

## Student Learning Outcomes

- **Know**: Understand the impact of sin.

- **Feel**: Resolve to combat sin in our lives.

- **Do**: Use the lessons from Genesis to grow spiritually.

## Support

- Series – Genesis – Foundational Book of the Bible (Mike Mazzalongo)

- Video – Lesson 19 – The Punishment of Cain

- Student Note Guide for Lesson 19

## Body of the Lesson

1.1   Cain's judgment
1.2   The way of Cain
1.3   Lessons

# Discussion Questions

Below are suggested questions to use during the guided discussion portion of the lesson. There are also suggested responses to questions to help students grasp the various concepts. These are provided to assist the discussion and are not considered as "right or wrong" responses.

## 1. Summarize the event of Cain's sin from Genesis 4.

Adam and Eve had two sons, Cain and Abel. Cain was a farmer while Abel was a shepherd. Both offered sacrifices to God from their efforts. Abel's was accepted but Cain's sacrifice was rejected by God. As a result, Cain became resentful and angry at Abel and killed him. As a result, God banished Cain from his family.

## 2. What was Cain's reaction to God's question regarding Abel and how does this relate to the immediate impact of sin on our relationship with God?

Cain lied and offered excuses (Genesis 4:9). In the same way, we also try to justify ourselves about our sins. This results in a separation between God and ourselves where we are unable to draw near to Him for prayer and worship.

## 3. Summarize Cain's punishment and its impact on him.

God pronounced a similar punishment to that of Adam. The ground would no longer yield its strength to him. He was also banished from his previous relationship with God. He would now become a wanderer on earth. He would never again be at peace.

Cain recognizes his situation and impact and cries out to God for mercy. As a result, God provides a way that Cain would be protected from attack by other. However, he would always be seen as a reminder of the impact of sin.

## 4. Why did God allow intermarriage between family members and polygamy?

This was the only possible way in the early stages of man for populating the earth. Genetic mutation from intermarriage had not occurred yet. As for polygamy, it is true that God created marriage to be for only one man and one woman. Sometimes, however, God allows practices that He does not specifically sanction. There is no indication that God approved of polygamy but He did allow it to occur for a time.

A point of note here. Throughout history man has tried to act on his own rather than rely on God's guidance and will. This is where we use the gifts of intellect and choice poorly. We try to reason based on our will rather than have faith in God's will. We will see in later lessons how this happened with Abraham as his lack of faith caused problems.

## 5. Read Genesis 4:17-22 and summarize the different ways the descendants of Cain changed life.

God allowed Cain to marry and have descendants. This continued God's command for man to populate the earth. The descendants of Adam's immediate family were given the abilities to develop in different ways. Jabal invented tents and specialized in the care of animals to accommodate a nomadic lifestyle. Jubal created musical instruments. Tubal-cain developed the ability to fabricate metal instruments.

## 6. Why does God allow the writers of scripture to include the sins and weaknesses of mankind?

The intent of this question is to bring about a greater understanding of the goodness and love of God. Answers to this will vary. Here are some suggested insights.

- By showing man's sin we see the contrast between our weaknesses and God's love and goodness.

- It shows that God continues to love us and is willing to accept us when we repent, regardless of the level or type of sin.

- To teach us that sin is evil and prevents us from being a part of God's holiness.

- To show the result of faith and repentance.

- It shows us that it is not possible for us to live pure lives and demonstrates our need for the substitutionary sacrifice of Jesus for our sins.

## 7. Read Genesis 3:11-13 and Genesis 4:9 and answer the following questions.

**What are the similarities between the reaction of Adam and Eve when God confronted them for their sin, and the reaction of Cain when he was confronted?**

Both offered excuses and tried to place the blame elsewhere. God brings about a direct understanding of the underlying sin (disobedience, doubt, pride, etc.) and punishes them.

**Defend the idea that if Adam and Eve or Cain had responded differently by repenting before God that God would have forgiven them rather than punish them.**

This is proven throughout scripture. In several places God forgave people for some of the most egregious sins. God forgave David for his sin with Bathsheba. God forgave Paul for his persecution of the early Christians. God forgave Peter for his denial of Jesus. God forgives us when we repent and turn to Him.

This does not remove the immediate consequences of our sin, but it does remove the ultimate consequence of separation from God.

**What does the example of Adam, Eve and Cain's reaction teach us?**

We must be willing to recognize and sincerely repent of our sins. When we do so, God will forgive us.

## 8. Compare Cain's statement in Genesis 4:13-14 and that of our Lord in Matthew 27:46.

By Cain's statement we can infer that he recognized that the greater part of His punishment would be he could no longer interact with God directly. This was a direct consequence of his sin. In like manner, when Jesus took on our sins upon Himself, He suffered the same consequence of being separated from His father.

Sin separates us from God at the spiritual as well as physical level. We cannot honestly or acceptably come to God in prayer except to beg for forgiveness and mercy. We cannot come into the presence of God to worship until we repent.

**A point to note:** God made allowance for Cain by not destroying him when Cain recognized his sin and situation. God also makes allowance for us if we are living faithfully and repent when we recognize our sin (1 John 1:7-9).

## 9. How can you use this lesson to grow spiritually and help others come into a relationship with Jesus?

Sin impacts us and others both directly and indirectly. From Adam through today we continue to sin by disobeying God. There are many reasons but ultimately it is still disobedience. As a result, we too face separation from God and death. But in His infinite love, God made a way for us to return to Him and receive forgiveness. This is through the ultimate sacrifice of Jesus. The consequences of sin on our lives and the lives of others are still present, but the ultimate consequence of spiritual death has been removed.

# Lesson 20 – Seed of Promise

### Teaching Strategy

The focus of this lesson is to identify and trace the lineage of those who will eventually deliver the Seed of Promise to mankind. Of special note in this lesson is the faithfulness of God to continue with His promise of a redeemer.

### Student Learning Outcomes

- **Know**: Understand the love God has for His creation as shown through His faithfulness to His promise of a redeemer.

- **Feel**: Appreciate God's faithfulness.

- **Do**: Use the information of God's faithfulness to build the virtue of faithfulness in our lives.

### Support

- Series – Genesis – Foundational Book of the Bible (Mike Mazzalongo)

- Video – Lesson 20 – Seed of Promise

- Student Note Guide for Lesson 20

### Body of the Lesson

1.1    The seed of promise
1.2    The generations of Adam
1.3    Lessons

## Discussion Questions

Below are suggested questions to use during the guided discussion portion of the lesson. There are also suggested responses to questions to help students grasp the various concepts. These are provided to assist the discussion and are not considered as "right or wrong" responses.

## 1. What is the relationship between God's promise in Genesis 3:15 and the birth of Seth in Genesis 4:25-26?

God promised that from the seed of man, specifically through Eve that one day a deliverer would be born Who would defeat Satan and redeem man. With the death of Abel and the banishment of Cain, it seemed like no suitable person remained to maintain the hope. God gave Seth as an answer. This shows that in spite of Satan's worst efforts, God's will was not thwarted.

**Note:** Satan is powerful and has many tools to use against God, through us. However, never forget that Satan is a created being and is therefore not more powerful than God. Yes, he is more powerful than we are, however, this is why we put our faith in God.

This promise was eventually fulfilled in Jesus. In Him we now have the hope that was lost in sin. To God be the glory for His love and faithfulness to us!

## 2. What is meant by the statement in Genesis 4:26, "Then men began to call upon the name of the Lord"?

With Seth a renewal of both faith and worship of God was experienced in that ancient society.

## 3. Why would Genesis record in detail the lineage from Adam forward?

This shows how God continued to maintain His guidance for bringing about a redeemer, as promised. By having the details of names, dates and events, we can verify history. This provides further proof of the truth of the writer's words.

## 4. What is meant by the description of Enoch of, "He walked with God"? What is the implication for us?

Walking with God means we are faithful to His will. The result was that Enoch did not die (Geneses 5:21-24).

The implication is that as we walk with God, we too will be rewarded by God. We may die physically, but our soul will be with God for eternity.

A mark of spiritual maturity is when we realize and accept that God is faithful to His promise of redeeming us.

## 5. What is the meaning of "type" as used to describe Enoch and Elijah?

Enoch and Elijah did not suffer physical death. This is perhaps pointing to Jesus who, although physically died, was resurrected from the dead. Enoch and Elijah were not the promised redeemer, but they were faithful to their role as prophets of God and in their direct accent to heaven pointed to the fact that Jesus, also, would ascend to heaven.

## 6. What was the major result of Noah's salvation from the flood?

Yet again we see God making provision for the promised redeemer. Although, as Genesis describes it, every thought of man was evil, God saw the faithfulness of Noah and blessed him for it. The blessing was saving Noah and his family so that mankind would continue, and the promise of God would be fulfilled.

## 7. How can you use this lesson to grow spiritually and help others come into a relationship with Jesus?

God is faithful to His word. He promises to redeem those faithful to Him. We can trust that promise because we see throughout man's history as recorded in scripture that God kept His promise. Sometimes it seemed dark and hopeless, that Satan was winning. No greater example of perceived hopelessness and Satan's victory than the dark hour of the death of Jesus. Yet even in this, God's plan was being fulfilled. A sacrifice for sin was required. Jesus not only became the sacrifice, but the gateway to salvation. Without the death and His resurrection, we would have no hope of redemption.

# Lesson 21 – The Times of Noah

### Teaching Strategy

The focus of this lesson is to review the condition of man and the world prior to the great flood. Of special note in this lesson is information about Noah, the condition of society in which he lived and God's reasons for destroying the world.

### Student Learning Outcomes

- **Know**: Understand the condition of man and how God provided a promised redeemer.

- **Feel**: Develop an appreciation for God's faithfulness.

- **Do**: Use the information gained from Genesis to strengthen our faith.

### Support

- Series – Genesis – Foundational Book of the Bible (Mike Mazzalongo)

- Video – Lesson 21 – The Times of Noah

- Student Note Guide for Lesson 21

### Body of the Lesson

1.1     Noah
1.2     The condition of man
1.3     Lessons

## Discussion Questions

Below are suggested questions to use during the guided discussion portion of the lesson. There are also suggested responses to questions to help students grasp the various concepts. These are provided to assist the discussion and are not considered as "right or wrong" responses.

**1. Read Mathew 24:37-39. Other than the purpose of Jesus making this statement about His return, what else could be significant about this passage?**

The intent is to establish the truth of the account of the flood from Genesis. There are records of a global flood in religious writings all around the world yet many still see this as a myth. They believe in Jesus as a historical figure and as the Son of God yet doubt other writings in scripture. If Satan can cause someone to disbelieve any part of scripture then the entirety of scripture is called into question, including, ironically, Satan himself. Whether one believes in Satan or not, to deny God is to be lost.

By recounting this information as a statement of fact, we can believe the event was true as described in scripture and study it as a guide for our attitude towards God, His word, and His warning to be prepared for our Lord's coming.

**2. State some facts about Noah as recorded in Genesis 5.**

Noah was the son of Lamech. He was designated by God to be the one who would bring relief (meaning he was the one that would continue the promise from God of a redeemer). The relief spoken of here would be relief from the curse of sin that would come through Jesus. Noah was the father of Shem, Ham and Japheth.

## 3. What was the impact of the "Sons of God" marrying the daughters of man?

They produced offspring referred to as the, "mighty men who were of old, men or renown." They were super powerful, wicked and raised the level of evil and violence in the world. God placed a judgment upon man where he would no longer live past than 120 years (Genesis 6:1-4).

## 4. Review the following scriptures, compare them with Genesis 6:5-6 and discuss the implications of these for us.

- Luke 17:26-27 – Preoccupation with physical appetites (materialism)
- Genesis 6:2 – Satanic activity in the physical realm
- Hebrews 11:7 – General unbelief
- Jude 14-15 – Ungodly behavior
- Genesis 6:11-13 – Widespread violence

These scriptures summarize much of what we see in our world today. We read in Genesis 6:5-6 that man had grown so wicked that everything he thought of and did was wicked. As a result, God was sorry He had created man.

The implication is that when we continue to turn from God or reject the opportunity to turn to God, we make God sorrowful. In His sorrow He will act to eventually remove us. Jesus promised He will return at a time only God the Father knows. When He returns, He will pronounce judgment upon the wicked of eternal separation and punishment and for the righteous (those in Christ), a reward including eternity in the presence of God.

**Note:** Some versions use the word "repent" instead of sorrow. This is not that God sinned, but rather changes His attitude toward man. He doesn't lose His love for man but does regret the condition of man that clearly will not turn back to Him. God doesn't reject us, we reject Him.

**5. Read Genesis 6:22, 7:5, 7:9; 7:16 and use only one word to describe Noah and the implication of these words for us.**

There might be many words used but the key word being looked for is "obedient." The implication is that if we are obedient to God's will then we also will be saved. Our obedience is not earning salvation but acting upon our faith, just as Noah did.

**6. How can you use this lesson to grow spiritually and help others come into a relationship with Jesus?**

God is faithful to His promise both to destroy wickedness and to save those who are righteous. The only way we can be made righteous before God is through Jesus. As noted in this lesson, Noah obeyed God to the best of his ability. He was not perfect, but because of his faithfulness God saved him. That is true for us as well. We are not perfect, but we recognize God as our creator and redeemer. We do the best we can to obey Him. We resolve to live according to the teachings of Jesus and honor Him as Lord.

# Lesson 22 – The Building of the Ark

## Teaching Strategy

The focus of this lesson is to review the building of the Ark. Of special note in this lesson are the similarities between the Ark and the Church.

## Student Learning Outcomes

- **Know**: Understand how God provides for those faithful to Him.

- **Feel**: Believe God will save the faithful as seen in the salvation of those in the Ark and those in the Church.

- **Do**: Strive to remain faithful.

## Support

- Series – Genesis – Foundational Book of the Bible (Mike Mazzalongo)

- Video – Lesson 22 – The Building of the Ark

- Student Note Guide for Lesson 22

## Body of the Lesson

1.1     The Ark
1.2     God's judgment and promise to Noah
1.3     Lessons

# Discussion Questions

Below are suggested questions to use during the guided discussion portion of the lesson. There are also suggested responses to questions to help students grasp the various concepts. These are provided to assist the discussion and are not considered as "right or wrong" responses.

## 1. Summarize Genesis 6:14-16 and answer the following questions.

God gives Noah specific instructions to build a floating vessel in which he, his family and air breathing animals would be saved from the flood.

**Why did God provide the details for building the Ark?**

God knew what was to happen and what would be needed for their survival.

**What was Noah's reaction and the final result?**

Noah did what God commanded and was saved as God promised.

**What is the implication of this passage for us?**

God will make a way to save the faithful people who obey Him.

## 2. Genesis 6:9 states that Noah walked with God. This is the same language in Genesis 5:27 that describes Enoch. Why was Noah not taken as Enoch was?

God had a different plan for Noah. God did not destroy Noah along with the rest due to his righteousness. It was through Noah that the promise of a redeemer would come.

NOTE: It is up to God how He rewards and punishes. He knows His plans for us and how to best carry them out. Our role is to do the best we can to be faithful. God will keep His promise to reward us beyond our ability to comprehend.

### 3. What are some lessons we can learn from Genesis 6:17-22.

There are several lessons in these verses.  The intent of the question is to show that God is in control of His creation and knows what is best for us.

- God is the one who destroyed the life that He created.  He was in full control.  Man had destroyed his own innocence but God brought about the ultimate end of that generation. (vs. 17)

- God will ultimately act against evil and on behalf of His righteous people. (vs. 17)

- God confirms His promise of a redeemer by specifically establishing a covenant with Noah. (vs. 18)

- God knows our needs and provides for them. (vs. 19-21)

- Noah did as God commanded and was saved.  It was through Noah's obedience that God considered him righteous. (vs. 22)

### 4. How do the following statements show the Ark was type for the Church today?

- One Ark/one church

- Safety only in the Ark/Safety only in the church

- Only one way into the ark/only one way into the church (Christ – John 14:6)

- Those in the ark are alive through the water/Those in the church are alive through the water of baptism

- The ark carries them to the next life; a re-created earth/The church carries us to the new heavens and new earth.

- Only believers were in the ark/Only believers are in the church.

- The ark was laughed at and seemed irrelevant before the flood/The church seems irrelevant before the judgment.

- The ark was built by those who believed and obeyed God's promises/The church is built by those who believe and obey God's promises.

- God provided for those who built and lived in it / God provides for the establishing of His church and preserves it through the catastrophes of this life.

- The ark was necessary because the flood did come. The church is necessary because the judgment will surely come with Jesus' return.

## 5. How can you use this lesson to grow spiritually and help others come into a relationship with Jesus?

God has always provided salvation for the faithful. Those not faithful have always faced ultimate judgment and destruction. Many begin their spiritual journey to avoid punishment. However, as we grow in knowledge of God as well as His love and grace, we develop dedication and the desire to be what He wants us to be. This story shows us the importance of our membership in the Church through which we effectively serve God, but the type of Ark through which we will avoid the next catastrophe for those who refuse to believe the gospel. We do not earn righteousness but are made righteous through the blood of Christ (Romans 3:22; 5:1-11).

# Lesson 23 – Flood Details

## Teaching Strategy

The focus of this lesson is to review the details of final preparation and physical details of the flood. Of special note in this lesson is the result of both man's disobedience and obedience.

## Student Learning Outcomes

- **Know**: Understand the consequences of obedience and disobedience to God.

- **Feel**: Value the importance of obedience to God.

- **Do**: Resolve to live faithfully according to God's will.

## Support

- Series – Genesis – Foundational Book of the Bible (Mike Mazzalongo)

- Video – Lesson 23 – Flood Details

- Student Note Guide for Lesson 23

## Body of the Lesson

1.1     God breaks His silence
1.2     The flood
1.3     Lessons

# Discussion Questions

Below are suggested questions to use during the guided discussion portion of the lesson. There are also suggested responses to questions to help students grasp the various concepts. These are provided to assist the discussion and are not considered as "right or wrong" responses.

## 1. Why did God wait 120 years between the pronouncement of His judgment and instructions to Noah and the actual flood? What are the implications for us?

The delay gave man time to repent. During this time Noah not only built the Ark but was both a living and vocal herald of the impending destruction as well as the need to repent (2 Peter 2:5). It also gave Noah time to physically finish the Ark, gather resources and for the animals to be assembled by God.

**Note**: Both Jesus and Peter refer to the flood as a historic event (Matthew 24:36-44; Luke 17:26-27). This indicates that it was not a myth but happened exactly as scriptures describe the event.

One implication is that God is patient wanting no one to perish (2 Peter 3:9). We work according to God's timeline. He knows His plans for us. Our role is to faithfully carry out His will and not grow faint in doing so. We also learn that God will keep His promise in His time, not ours. We must be ready. Noah gave warning and the signs were there for men to see. Today, God gives us warning through His word. We can see how this world is spinning towards destruction due to the evil all around us. As God clearly states, the end will come when He is ready. Our role is to be prepared now. We will not have the opportunity to repent when our Lord returns nor will we be able to say that we didn't know.

## 2. Why did God make the distinctions between clean and unclean animals to enter the Ark?

The inclusion of all types of animals would continue the balance of nature after the flood. God was providing for this to happen. Also, clean and unclean animals would provide for the establishment of the sacrificial system He would later put into place.

## 3. Summarize Genesis 7:10-24 and state the significance of how God brings about the flood.

The flood was a worldwide destruction leading to the death of all life on the land and in the air. Rain alone could not produce such a catastrophic flood in a 40-day period hence the release of subterranean water. The 40-day period ensured that a complete destruction would occur.

## 4. What were the root causes of the flood?

Man rejected God's will looking only to his own pleasures and desires (Genesis 6:5). Man had taken a perfect environment and through sin, destroyed it. God, as creator and sustainer of life, chose to keep His promise of a redeemer while also completely destroying and then restoring life. We do not know the exact timespan before the events of the flood but we do know that it was long enough for man to repent. However, man continued to reject God, forcing Him to act.

The implication for us is that we must strive to do God's will. In doing so we serve God as He wishes, avoid catastrophe in our lives and receive the blessings that accompany faithfulness.

**Note**: All during the period leading up to the flood Noah would have been challenged in His faith. The physical strain of building the Ark while also providing for his family, the spiritual and emotional strain of knowing destruction was coming and having to endure the pressure from doubters and unbelievers around him would be opportunities to disobey. Yet, Noah endured the test and was rewarded for his faithfulness (Hebrews 11:7).

## 5. Compare the 40 days of the flood to the 40 years of wandering by Israel (Numbers 13:30-37; 32:13).

The 40 days of flooding served to remove those that brought about this catastrophe by their disobedience. In like manner, the 40 years of wandering in the desert served to remove from God's people those who had been disobedient to God.

**Note**: Noah and his family were spared due to their faithfulness. Joshua and Caleb were spared for the same reason. We too will be spared destruction at the return of Jesus if we remain faithful.

## 6. How can you use this lesson to grow spiritually and help others come into a relationship with Jesus?

God keeps His promises. He promises destruction on those that reject Him and has done so throughout history. Sometimes the destruction comes after a long period and even seems that it will not occur, but God eventually punishes wickedness.
He promises salvation to those that accept Him and live faithfully.
It seems at times that this takes a long period, but God always keeps His promises.

God requires obedience or the sincere effort at obedience. Our role is to strive to live faithfully. When we see that we have not done so, we must immediately repent. God will forgive as we have seen time and time again.

# Lesson 24 – Effects of the Great Flood

## Teaching Strategy

The focus of this lesson is to review the effects of the great flood on the earth and human existence. Of special note in this lesson is God's renewed covenant with Noah.

## Student Learning Outcomes

- **Know**: Understand the love God has for His creation as shown through His faithfulness to His promise of a redeemer.

- **Feel**: Appreciate God's faithfulness.

- **Do**: Use the information of God's faithfulness to build faithfulness in our lives.

## Support

- Series – Genesis – Foundational Book of the Bible (Mike Mazzalongo)

- Video – Lesson 24 – Effects of the Great Flood

- Student Note Guide for Lesson 24

## Body of the Lesson

1.1     Results of the flood
1.2     God and Noah after the flood
1.3     Lessons

# Discussion Questions

Below are suggested questions to use during the guided discussion portion of the lesson. There are also suggested responses to questions to help students grasp the various concepts. These are provided to assist the discussion and are not considered as "right or wrong" responses.

## 1. Summarize key points from Genesis 8:1-14.

- God shifts His focus from the destruction of the earth to Noah and the others in the Ark.

- God stops the waters from the earth and sky and begins to dry up the land.

- The water recedes over a 150-day period.

- The Ark rests on Mount Ararat.

- Noah sends out a raven and dove to determine the condition of the earth.

- The dove finally does not return letting Noah know that the earth is now dry enough to be habitable.

- After a year in the Ark, Noah removes its cover and sees dry land.

## 2. What are some major effects of the flood on the earth that we can still see today?

- The continents were formed along with the oceans.

- The land was reshaped to form mountains, valleys, major rivers and bodies of water.

- The earth's crust now held fossil records of life before the flood.

- The atmosphere and ecological patterns were changed.

## 3. Summarize the continued faithfulness of God to Noah as seen in Genesis 8:15-22 and discuss the implications for us.

The intent of this question is to show that God remains faithful to His promise.

God commands Noah and the others to go out of the Ark and inhabit the new world. Noah does so and makes an offering of clean animals to God. God then extends His covenant with Noah promising never to destroy the earth by water again. He also implements the seasons and their effects to sustain the new life. God further implements the beginnings of law by placing a prohibition and punishment for the taking of life.

Major implications are that today we live under a system of government and law designed to regulate society, protect the innocent and punish those guilty of violations. God would later provide details for His people through the law given to Moses. Many of our laws today are drawn from this initial prohibition of murder and the punishment required for this crime. We must also be good stewards of our world. Instead of having dominion over creation, we are now co-inhabitants and must be good stewards of our environment.

## 4. How can you use this lesson to grow spiritually and help others come into a relationship with Jesus?

Genesis records that God "remembered" Noah and those in the Ark. It isn't that God forgot them for a period. Rather, He brought His focus back to them.

In similar ways, we are promised that, as children of God and in Christ, God remembers our sins no more (Isaiah 43:25; 2 Corinthians 5:19, among many other references). It isn't that God develops amnesia, it means that He will not hold us accountable for them. He does this because He placed the accountability for our sins on Jesus. This is why Jesus had to die. He paid the price for sin imposed by God. Once the price had been paid (Jesus' perfect life given in exchange for the sins of mankind), God now no longer holds those in Christ guilty and thus subject to condemnation and eternal death (Romans 5:1-11).

# Lesson 25 – The Rainbow Covenant

## Teaching Strategy

The focus of this lesson is to review God's rededication to His promise to redeem man. Of special note in this lesson is the promise to Noah guaranteeing the survival of man, the giving of the rainbow as a sign of that promise and how the descendants of Noah impacted mankind as they populated the new world.

## Student Learning Outcomes

- **Know**: Understand how God continues His promise to redeem man through the early life of Noah and his descendants following the flood.

- **Feel**: Recognize in our own lives how God provides for our survival for eternity through Jesus.

- **Do**: Continue our commitment to faithfulness and spiritual growth.

## Support

- Series – Genesis – Foundational Book of the Bible (Mike Mazzalongo)

- Video – Lesson 25 – The Rainbow Covenant

- Student Note Guide for Lesson 25

## Body of the Lesson

1.1  The rainbow Covenant
1.2  The sons of Noah
1.3  Lessons

# Discussion Questions

Below are suggested questions to use during the guided discussion portion of the lesson. There are also suggested responses to questions to help students grasp the various concepts. These are provided to assist the discussion and are not considered as "right or wrong" responses.

## 1. Summarize Genesis 9:7-17 and discuss its significance.

God commands Noah and the others to leave the Ark and populate the new world. He reestablishes His promise to Noah for the survival and redemption of man. Since the world has now changed and man would be subject to a harsh environment, God offers reassurance to assuage their potential fears of another flood or other catastrophic destruction by creating a rainbow as a reminder to God and a sign to man that He would not destroy the world by flood again.

**Note**: The rainbow phenomena appears after the rain as the emerging sun shines through the clouds. It's as if God was saying, "See, there's no need to fear." A rainbow after a storm serves as a metaphor for life. We all face storms, but God has promised to see us through (See Psalm 29).

## 2. Discuss the events of Genesis 9:20-23 and show the similarities between this event and the immediate consequences of Adam and Eve's original sin.

Noah, in a period of weakness, becomes drunk and falls asleep in his tent naked. His youngest son Ham sees his father in this condition and apparently, as a sign of disrespect and possible rebellion discusses it with his brothers. His brothers respectfully cover Noah. As a result, Noah pronounces a judgment against Ham that he and his descendants will serve his other brothers. This is the first recorded sin in the new world.

The similarities will vary but note that Adam and Eve immediately recognized their nakedness and shame after their sin. Now Noah in his weakness is naked and exposed. Sin leaves us naked and shamed before God.

Ham had a choice to honor his father but possibly chose instead to elevate himself before the others. In like fashion, Satan used the element of false pride to cause Adam and Eve to try to elevate themselves. Pride was the core element in the sin of Adam and Eve and likely at the heart of Ham's sin.

## 3. Explain the characteristics and contributions of each of Noah's sons and their significance.

**Shem** – Shem fathered the nation through which Jesus would eventually be born into. God, through Shem, would sustain His promise.

> **Note**: Some versions place Shem as the oldest son. Others have Japheth as the oldest. In many cultures, especially in the Eastern and Jewish cultures, it is through the first-born son that the family is provided for. In a much larger and grander way, Jesus is the first born of many sons. It is through Jesus that we are provided for (Romans 8:29). Although Shem may not have been the first born, God chose to deliver the promised redeemer through his lineage.

**Ham** – Ham and his descendants were to develop methods and skills in cultivation, tools, weaving, medicines and medical procedures, math, banking, commerce and writing. All these would be used to enable social structure, survival and see to the general wellbeing of others.

> **Note:** Although the judgment of Noah was that Ham and his descendants were to serve, Jesus elevates the role of a servant and encourages us to serve. There is greatness in serving when done for the right purposes.

**Japheth** – Japheth and his descendants were the philosophers, artisans and scientists. They were to "dwell in tents" noting fellowship or sharing with the others the knowledge and skills they developed. This crossed over to all races enriching and adding quality of life to all.

**4. How can you use this lesson to grow spiritually and help others come into a relationship with Jesus?**

God knows that we need opportunities to thrive spiritually, physically and philosophically/emotionally. Through the descendants of Noah, He provided these opportunities for us in many ways. He especially provides for our greatest need, redemption from our sins, through His first born, Jesus Christ.

# Lesson 26 – The Table and the Tower

### Teaching Strategy

The focus of this lesson is to review the biblical record of how nations were originally established. Of special note in this lesson is how God dealt with man's rebellion against populating the earth.

### Student Learning Outcomes

- **Know**: Understand how God continues to be faithful to His promise.

- **Feel**: Value the importance of following God's will.

- **Do**: Use the information gained from Genesis to strengthen our faith.

### Support

- Series – Genesis – Foundational Book of the Bible (Mike Mazzalongo)

- Video – Lesson 26 – The Table and the Tower

- Student Note Guide for Lesson 26

### Body of the Lesson

1.1     The Table of nations
1.2     The Tower of Babel
1.3     Lessons

## Discussion Questions

Below are suggested questions to use during the guided discussion portion of the lesson. There are also suggested responses to questions to help students grasp the various concepts. These are provided to assist the discussion and are not considered as "right or wrong" responses.

## 1. Summarize the events from Genesis 8 and 9.

The intent of this question is to continue the flow of history following the flood into the next phase of man's existence.

The flood that destroyed all life outside the Ark began to subside. Noah, his family and the animals leave the Ark and begin to repopulate the new world. This new world would be vastly different than the world Noah left. The terrain, environment and weather patterns would be completely changed. God promises that He will not destroy life by flood again and places a rainbow in the sky as a symbol of His promise.

Noah plants a vineyard and becomes drunk from the wine he produced. He falls asleep naked in his tent. His youngest son, Ham, sees him and rather than covering Noah, speaks about it to his brothers. The others cover Noah. As a result of Ham's dishonor, Noah pronounces judgment against him stating that he and his descendants will be servants to his brothers.

The chapter ends at this point with a statement of the death of Noah after 950 years.

## 2. What is the difference between the genealogical listing in Genesis 10 and that of Adam, and what is the purpose of this difference?

Adam's genealogical listing focuses on people. Noah's genealogical listing focuses on people, nations and civilizations. We also see the characteristics of the people. This is a wider survey of how the nations were formed.

## 3. Summarize the events of Genesis 11 and discuss their significance.

As man's population grew, they all spoke the same language.  Instead of dispersing and populating the earth, they chose to settle in the area of Shinar.  They decided to build a city and tower.  This went against God's intent for them to disperse and populate the earth.

God sees the people's unified rebellion and as a result confuses their languages.  This results in a stoppage of their efforts to build the tower and forces a dispersion.

> **Note**:  God uses language to drive them apart.  Later, in Acts 2, God will use language to bring man together with an understanding of His will for our salvation.

The remainder of Genesis 11 continues with the further record of key ancestors of the lineage of Shem that would lead to the birth of Jesus, the promised redeemer.

There are several significant elements to this biblical account.

> **Note**:  There may be other items noted by students.  Encourage them to add to this list what they see as additional items of significance.

- God puts down their rebellion by destroying their unity but not by destroying them.  There is no record of anyone being destroyed but rather they are dispersed.
- Languages and associated cultures are established.
- The world-wide population begins.
- The lineage of Jesus through Abram (Abraham) is recorded.

**4. How can you use this lesson to grow spiritually and help others come into a relationship with Jesus?**

The event of the Tower of Babel is just another example of how man fails to do God's will. God had promised not to destroy man again by flood and for man to move out to populate the earth. Man chose instead to use his own knowledge and skills to prevent God's will. In this case, a tower to "reach into the heavens". Throughout our history we have tried to go against God's will or to impose our efforts to take control.

The use of this information shows that try as man might, God remains in control and remains faithful to His promises. Even though man continues to rebel, God moves us toward His plan. We must seek God's way in all things thus showing our faith in Him and love for Him by our submission and obedience. God knows what is best for us in both the end result and the process to achieve it.

# Lesson 27 – Abraham – Father of a Nation

## Teaching Strategy

The focus of this lesson is to introduce Abraham as God continues His covenant with man. Of special note in this lesson is the calling of Abraham and his initial trip to Egypt.

## Student Learning Outcomes

- **Know**: See the promise to Abraham as an example of God's faithfulness to us.
- **Feel**: Value the faithfulness of God.
- **Do**: Use the information gained from God's promise to Abraham to strengthen our faith.

## Support

- Series – Genesis – Foundational Book of the Bible (Mike Mazzalongo)
- Video – Lesson 27 – Abraham: Father of a Nation
- Student Note Guide for Lesson 27

## Body of the Lesson

1.1     Abraham
1.2     Abraham in Egypt
1.3     Lessons

# Discussion Questions

Below are suggested questions to use during the guided discussion portion of the lesson. There are also suggested responses to questions to help students grasp the various concepts. These are provided to assist the discussion and are not considered as "right or wrong" responses.

## 1. Summarize Genesis 12:1-9 and discuss how it serves as a model for Christians today.

Abraham (Abram) received a direct call from God to leave the country where he lived and go to an unnamed place. God also makes a promise to Abraham that He will bless him for doing so. This blessing included that he would become a great nation, a great man, he would be protected by God, and, as history reveals, the redeemer would be from his lineage.

There are several elements that serve as a model for Christians today. First, one must wonder why God chose Abraham from among the others. There's no direct reason stated but it is obvious that Abraham demonstrated a significant level of faith (Hebrews 11:8-12). Abraham was given a choice to obey God or to remain in his perceived place of safety. Although Abraham did not always make good choices, he did on this occasion. As seekers of God's will we initially may have little faith, or even knowledge of God but God doesn't demand great faith in our initial response.

Today, a person is given the choice to obey God's calling to obey the gospel or remain in their current situation. When we obey God, we begin a lifetime journey with many unknown pathways culminating in the ultimate blessing of redemption and eternity with God. Our submission to God, like Abraham, is an initial test of our faith. Like Abraham, however, our faith will grow as we come to know God more, develop a deeper love for Him and continue in our obedience.

Jesus makes a statement related to our calling that is very similar to the choice Abraham had to make. In Luke 14 we have the record of Jesus' statement concerning the cost of discipleship. He requires that we forsake all in our commitment to follow Him. If we do not, then we are not considered worthy to become a disciple. To one not converted to Jesus this seems like a disproportionate exchange. But a disciple grows to understand how much Jesus gave so we could have salvation. That clarifies the nature of the exchange in God's favor.

> **Note**: Joshua 24:2 records that Abraham's family were pagans. This adds an interesting element to why God chose Abraham from among others of other nations that may have appeared to be more faithful. Isaiah 51:1-2 describes Abraham as "the rock from which you were hewn." Abraham possessed the raw materials God would shape to become the father of a great nation. It took

a lifetime to achieve but in the end, God prevailed because Abraham was obedient. We too possess the raw materials God can use to achieve His purpose. We must submit to His will and allow Him to shape us into servants He can use.

## 2. Summarize Genesis 12:10-20. Why, after all that God had shown and promised to Abraham, did he go to Egypt, and what is the implication for us?

The Bible record does not tell us specifically all that Abraham thought as he chose to journey to Egypt. It does state there was a famine in the land. This likely brought hardship on him. In his immature faith he may have felt he had to make the effort to save his family. This was a departure from his faith in the promise from God to protect and provide for him. Egypt seemed to be an easy way out of the situation.

Abraham compounded the bad choice by lying about the identity of his wife. This brought distress upon the people of Egypt and shame upon Abraham. Although on the surface it seemed Abraham made a good choice in going to Egypt, it was a short-term reprieve. God intervened by causing plagues on Pharaoh and his household showing them that there was a problem with Abraham and his people. Ironically, Pharaoh rebukes Abraham for his deceit and lack of faith in God.

God gives us choices in how we serve Him. We must strive to make good choices using His will as revealed in scripture to grow and maintain our faithfulness.

### 3. How can you use this lesson to grow spiritually and help others come into a relationship with Jesus?

When we submit to God in obedient faith, we begin to receive the blessings of salvation. Our faith begins small and should grow as we come to know, love and obey our Lord even more. Along this journey we are tested in ways to serve that can weaken or even defeat our faith. We must be aware of this and resolve to stand firm. Satan wants us to fail and use a variety of measures to bring this about. Some of the measures may seem like good choices at first, but we must always examine how any action affects our obedience to God's will. If we find ourselves acting contrary to God's will then we must take action to regroup and return to compliance. We might know how to bring this about ourselves or it might take the loving discipline of others to help us.

# Lesson 28 – Abraham and Lot

## Teaching Strategy

The focus of this lesson is to review the events following Abraham and Lot's return from Egypt. Of special note in this lesson is the forgiveness of God when we return to him.

## Student Learning Outcomes

- **Know**: Understand the impact of faithfulness to our Lord.

- **Feel**: Appreciate that God's faithfulness remains despite our mistakes.

- **Do**: Use the information gained from Genesis to strengthen our faith.

## Support

- Series – Genesis – Foundational Book of the Bible (Mike Mazzalongo)

- Video – Lesson 28 – Abraham and Lot

- Student Note Guide for Lesson 28

## Body of the Lesson

1.1    Abraham's return
1.2    God renews His promise
1.3    Lessons

# Discussion Questions

Below are suggested questions to use during the guided discussion portion of the lesson. There are also suggested responses to questions to help students grasp the various concepts. These are provided to assist the discussion and are not considered as "right or wrong" responses.

**1. Summarize the events of Genesis 13 with emphasis on the reason and reaction of Abraham's offer to Lot.**

Abraham and Lot returned from Egypt to their former location in Bethel. Both families had great wealth gained from their time in Egypt. There is conflict between the two families because of the strain on the resources to maintain their herds. There are other peoples in the area as well. Abraham offers Lot the choice of where to dwell. Abraham will go in the opposite direction so there will be no conflict. Lot chooses the area in the Jordan Valley. Abraham settled in the land of Canaan. As a result of the mode in which the offer was made and the choice of Lot, peace between the families is restored. All of this is brought about by Abraham's humble attitude. Following Abraham's return and the resolution of the conflict between the two families, God renews His promise to Abraham.

Given the eventual message from scripture, we now see from the teachings of our Lord regarding His Kingdom, that the land God promised to His people is symbolic of the spiritual kingdom which God will bless His people with forever. The physical land Abraham received was a desert and mountainous land, not the fertile valleys chosen by Lot. In a similar way, the earth in which we live offers many enticements while faithful service to our Lord has challenges that can draw us away. However, the physical world will someday be destroyed and we will reap the eternal blessings from being part of the spiritual kingdom of God.

**2. Read Romans 8:28 and discuss the possibility that God allowed the conflict between Abraham and Lot in order to bring about His renewed focus on Abraham. Also discuss how this applies to us today.**

Sometimes God allows situations to occur so that we learn more of God's will. Abraham and Lot became wealthy due to Abraham's deception in Egypt. The wealth they gained did not result in peace. The opposite occurred. In an act of wisdom, Abraham resolved the conflict. This allowed him to return his focus more so on God. We cannot clearly state that God brought about these events but certainly He took Abraham from where he now was and redirected him back into the way God wished for Him. The same occurs in our lives today. We stray from God's will, but God takes us from where we are when we return and continues to work in our lives.

**3. Share some examples from scripture where someone made a poor choice and departed from God's will but were restored.**
**How does this apply to us today?**

The intent of this question is to show that God is faithful to His people once they repent. There are multiple examples that may come out. Look for examples that show the attitude and action that demonstrate true repentance.

This affects us today because we also can see the forgiveness God grants when we repent and return to Him. Some may wish to share from their own lives an example where God forgive them.

## 4. How can you use this lesson to grow spiritually and help others come into a relationship with Jesus?

Never forget that God takes us back. There are many examples in scripture of God restoring an individual once they repented. Abraham is an example from the Old Testament. God made a promise to Abraham, but Abraham desired to make his own way rather than follow God's way. This resulted in consequences he had not foreseen. To his credit, he repented and followed God's directions. There would still be consequences that had to be dealt with as a result of his poor choices, yet God demonstrated His faithfulness by renewing His promise to Abraham.

In the New Testament, God continues this promise through the teachings of Jesus. An example of this is from Luke 15 in the series of parables about God's forgiveness, culminating in the parable of the Prodigal Son. Here, Jesus teaches us that if we repent and return, no matter the depths of depravity we've turned to, God, our loving Father will take us back and fully restore us. In a wonderful statement related to this, Luke 15:7 and 10 state that there is rejoicing in heaven over the sinner that repents. Later, in the book of 1 John 1, John teaches us that God will take us back and remove our sin because we are in Christ and repent. This offers tremendous hope.

We can trust God's word. God demonstrated faithfulness to His promise time and again through the examples we see in scripture. This historical proof offers us confident assurance that He will continue to be faithful to those who are His. We must make every effort to maintain our faithfulness, and when we fail, turn quickly and sincerely to the Father in repentance.

# Lesson 29 – Melchizedek

### Teaching Strategy

The focus of this lesson is on Melchizedek as a symbol for Christ. Of special note in this lesson is how Abraham is an example for us as he realized that it was God who granted him victory over his enemies and how Abraham expressed his humility by honoring Melchizedek and refusing honors for himself.

### Student Learning Outcomes

- **Know**: Comprehend Abraham as an example for the proper attitude towards blessings from God.

- **Feel**: Appreciate that it is God who blesses us and that we must in turn use those blessings to bless others.

- **Do**: Use the information gained from Genesis to strengthen our faith.

### Support

- Series – Genesis – Foundational Book of the Bible (Mike Mazzalongo)

- Video – Lesson 29 – Melchizedek: A "Type" for Christ

- Student Note Guide for Lesson 29

### Body of the Lesson

1.1     The Northeastern kings
1.1.1   The war
1.1.2   The rescue
1.1.3   Melchizedek
1.1.4   The king of Sodom
1.2     Lessons

## Discussion Questions

Below are suggested questions to use during the guided discussion portion of the lesson. There are also suggested responses to questions to help students grasp the various concepts. These are provided to assist the discussion and are not considered as "right or wrong" responses.

**1. Summarize the events of Genesis 4:1-16 that led to the war and rescue of Lot. Discuss any significance you see from this event.**

Scripture doesn't give us a specific timeline of when these events occurred but apparently society began to evolve with more human led social structures in the form of city-states. The leaders of these were referred to as kings. One such group from the northern region scattered around Sodom and Gomorrah were led by a king called Chedorlaomer. This group of city-states revolted against the northern kings resulting in them being attacked. During this war Lot was taken captive. A refugee from the fighting informed Abraham about Lot's capture. Abraham led a force to recapture Lot, his family and possessions.

This event shows that society had evolved into a form of government. This evolution was obviously not for those that followed God. It also shows that even though it's not stated, God was obviously with Abraham. Abraham went into battle with a relatively small group of fighters against battle hardened forces under the 5 northern kings. This would be seen in the blessing given by Melchizedek (verse 20). God's promise of protection to Abraham would be put to the test and God fulfilled His promise.

**2. Summarize the events of the appearance and blessing of Melchizedek from Genesis 14:17-20 and discuss its significance.**

After Abraham returns from the victory and rescue of Lot, Melchizedek, a priest of God, blesses Abraham. Abraham, in turn gives Melchizedek a tenth of his possessions.

The significance of this is that Abraham recognizes Melchizedek as a person worthy of honor due to his position as a priest of God. From Abraham accepting the blessing we can surmise that he recognized the person and position of Melchizedek.

## 3. How is Melchizedek a "type" for Christ?

He is the type for the eternal priesthood of Christ. We don't know the beginning or end of Melchizedek. Hebrews 7:1-10 discusses how Melchizedek is a type for Christ. Melchizedek in having no genealogy showing his beginning or end resembled the Son of God as a priest forever. He took a tenth of the spoils setting the standard for taking tithes from the descendants of Abraham. This action shows that he was considered greater than Abraham.

## 4. What is significant about Abraham refusing the reward offered by the King of Sodom? (Genesis 14:21-24)

Abraham wanted all the glory and credit for his victory to point to God. If he had taken any of the spoils from the King of Sodom then others may have thought that it was he, and not God that had achieved the victory.

Recall that as Abraham is introduced in Genesis 12:1-2, God states that He will bless Abraham so that he will become a blessing to others. Part of that blessing are the physical blessings and the honors Abraham received. Abraham recognized this and shifted the true honor to God. This is an example of Abraham's faithfulness to God.

**5. How can you use this lesson to grow spiritually and help others come into a relationship with Jesus?**

Abraham knew that it was God who gave him victory over his enemies. We too must recognize that it is God who saves us from our spiritual enemies.

Too many times we see examples in scripture and in the lives of those who take credit and honor for their successes rather than recognize these as a blessing from God. Some fail to recognize their need for salvation, somehow reasoning that they can save themselves, or due to the great things they may have achieved in their lives will somehow be worthy of favor from God.

Paul teaches us that all have sinned and fallen short (Genesis 3:23). He also teaches us that we cannot save ourselves, but it is by God's grace through faith that we are saved (Ephesians 2:8). We come into contact with that saving grace by acting upon our faith.

# Lesson 30 – The Gospel in the Old Testament

### Teaching Strategy

The focus of this lesson is to show the gospel in the Old Testament. Of special note in this lesson is how God reveals through Abraham the principle of salvation through faith.

### Student Learning Outcomes

- **Know**: Make the connection between Abraham's faith and God's expectation for our faith.

- **Feel**: Allow knowledge of God's faithfulness to inspire us to build a stronger faith.

- **Do**: Live in such a way that we are seen as faithful servants for God.

### Support

- Series – Genesis – Foundational Book of the Bible (Mike Mazzalongo)

- Video – Lesson 30 – The Gospel in the Old Testament Teaching Guide

- Student Note Guide for Lesson 30

### Body of the Lesson

1.1     Summary of Genesis 15
1.2     God's reassurance to Abraham
1.3     Lessons

## Discussion Questions

Below are suggested questions to use during the guided discussion portion of the lesson. There are also suggested responses to questions to help students grasp the various concepts. These are provided to assist the discussion and are not considered as "right or wrong" responses.

# 1. Summarize Genesis 15:1-6 and answer the following questions:

God makes a general statement to Abraham as the narrative begins. The general statement is a reminder of God's promise from Genesis 12:1-2. Abraham has returned from his rescue of Lot where he won a decisive victory over a much larger and trained force. It is natural that Abraham would be concerned that he has no heirs and that he and Sarah (Sarai) are getting older. God takes Abram outside where He shows him that his descendants will be more numerous than the stars. These descendants would come from Abraham directly and not from his distant relatives or servants.

**What can we learn from Abraham based on this event?**

There are times when our faith is weak; times when we don't understand or see God working in our lives. We must remember that God made a promise to us as His people, and He will keep that promise.

**How does the promise regarding Abram's descendants numbering more than the stars directly apply to us?**

We look at this as Abraham's direct descendants in a physical way. Don't discount the indirect descendants from a spiritual way. We are descendants of the promise as we are now part of God's spiritual Kingdom (Galatians 3:7-9).

**Why would God delay giving children to Abraham and Sarah and how does that apply to us?**

There are multiple reasons. (1) By waiting until they were well beyond the normal age for childbearing, even in that time, it shows that God brought it about. (2) Abraham had to go through a period of trial and testing to develop his faith.

In our faith journey we understand the power of God, our reliance on Him, and our need for prayer. All too often we ask for things as children desiring our will be done rather than God's. We look at our lives only with our existence or relief from issues in view. Sometimes the delay in answered prayer is for similar reasons as with Abraham. We too need to see that it is God working in our lives. We need to develop a stronger faith. We need to pray for God's will, even if the answer is not a relief of our current situation. We sometimes pray for the wrong things or in the wrong way (James 4:1-10). God will answer and provide but it is by His time and His will. Always remember that we are the servant and He is the Master. Our desire is to hear, "Well done good and faithful servant." (Matthew 25).

## 2. Discuss the significance of Genesis 15:7-19.

Abraham wants a sign from God. He hears God's promise and intellectually understands it. But he still wants tangible proof. Perhaps this is due to his continued weak condition of faith. God gives him a more direct object lesson of His covenant by telling Abraham to make a sacrifice with specific instructions. These illustrate the great cost (5 animals), the seriousness of breaking a promise, the delay Abraham must accept and continue to be faithful through, the associated suffering God's people would endure (a cleansing and testing), God's unilateral commitment to His promise (He passed through the animals, not Abraham), and that the scope of the promise would be universal.

The promise of God has immediate and future implications. God caused Abraham to prosper, even when Abraham was weak. This shows God's protection as well as faithfulness to Abraham and the promise. All too often we equate blessings with temporal (earthly) manifestations. We may feel that if we are not prosperous in some way then we are not as blessed as others.  These are faulty comparisons.  God's blessings, as is His promise, are spiritual and therefore eternal.  We are sometimes granted physical blessings but are always granted spiritual blessings.  Regardless of the nature of the blessings, we must remember the reason God blessed Abraham (Genesis 12:1-2) and apply that standard to our blessings.  We are blessed so that we can bless others.  Whether physical and/or spiritual we give God the glory and use those blessings to help others come to know and glorify God.

## 3. How do you define faith?

Answers will vary.  Certainly, we generally quote Hebrews 11:1. When we look at the list of those within that chapter, we see a pattern emerge which Abraham especially practiced.  First, we must come to know God.  Knowledge of God goes beyond simple mental acceptance.  It includes a higher level of awareness born out through our growing relationship with Him.  Secondly, as Abraham and the others listed in Hebrews 11, and the faithful of today, we must learn to grow in our trust of God.  Trust is borne out through seeing God fulfilling His promises and knowing He will continue to do so.  Third, we must obey God.  It does no good to know and trust God if we are not willing to obey Him.  Obedience is sometimes difficult, and we are at times deliberately and unknowingly disobedient.  God expects faithfulness in our effort to obey, we demonstrate this.

## 4. How can you use this lesson to grow spiritually and help others come into a relationship with Jesus?

Abraham found physical and spiritual salvation because of his faith.  This serves as a model for us.  We must develop faith and grow in this grace.  We will be successful in serving God through our faith.  As Hebrews 11:6 states, it is impossible to please God without faith.  Therefore, just as we have seen through Abraham and others, God will reward our faithfulness.

# Lesson 31 –
# Sarai and Hagar's Conflict/Abram and Circumcision

## Teaching Strategy

The focus of this lesson is to review the actions between Sarai and Hagar. Of special note in this lesson are the issues that occur when we try to bypass God's plan and take our own actions. Also, we see the continued faithfulness of God to Abraham.

## Student Learning Outcomes

- **Know**: Understand how God continues to be faithful to His promise.

- **Feel**: Value the importance of following God's will.

- **Do**: Use the information gained from Genesis to strengthen our faith.

## Support

- Series – Genesis – Foundational Book of the Bible (Mike Mazzalongo)

- Video – Lesson 31 – Sarai and Hagar's Conflict/Abram and Circumcision

- Student Note Guide for Lesson 31

## Body of the Lesson

1.1    Sarai's Solution
1.2    Hagar's promise
1.3    The Covenant renewed
1.4    The Covenant confirmed
1.5    The name change
1.6    Lessons

# Discussion Questions

Below are suggested questions to use during the guided discussion portion of the lesson. There are also suggested responses to questions to help students grasp the various concepts. These are provided to assist the discussion and are not considered as "right or wrong" responses.

**1. Discuss what was evidently missing from Sarai's solution to God's delay in providing an heir to Abraham and how this relates to our life.**

The key element missing from Sarai's solution was her faith. She was impatient to have the promise fulfilled. She decided to act on her own rather than continue to trust in God's promise. Her weakened faith led her to resolve the situation her way rather than God's way.

We sometimes take the same attitude. We know that God promises to hear our prayers and care for us as His children, however, in our incomplete or imperfect faith we seek our own solution or grow impatient for any solution to our needs. Unfortunately, in this condition we are seeking "My will" rather than "Thy will."

**2. How did Sarai's actions fall short of God's will? How does this relate to us?**

She violated God's will that marriage was an exclusive relationship between the husband and wife. Sarai brought in Hagar which was against God's will.

Sarai violated God's will by taking charge of the situation herself in seeking a worldly solution rather than a godly one. She doubted God's promise because it was different than her understanding of the natural way of conceiving and delivering a child.

God's plan for marriage is an exclusive relationship between a man and a woman. We must not bring others into this intimate relationship, no matter the circumstances.

Furthermore, we must allow God to work things out for us. We contribute but rely on His will to guide us. We must not impose our will over God's will. One of the results of the Spirit acting in our lives is patience (Galatians 5:22).

## 3. Describe Hagar's faith as compared to Sarai's? What can we learn from this?

Sarai did not trust or obey God in her actions. This indicated a weak, to almost non-existent faith.

Although we don't have a direct statement in Genesis 16 about Hagar's faith, we can see its evidence. First, she obeyed the angel of the Lord when instructed to return to Sarai. She also obeyed the command to name her son, Ishmael. Her statement in verse 13 shows a belief and trust in God, key components of faith.

Sometimes in our lives we also take matters into our own hands rather than seek God's will. When this happens, it results in disaster at some point in time. As with Sarai, God has a wonderful way of taking a situation and redirecting it back to His will. We might not see this in the consequences of our mistakes, but the more we continue to seek God's will, the more evident it will become that God continues to use us for His purpose.

## 4. What was at the core of God giving Abram a new name?

God gave Abram a new identity by changing his name to Abraham. The new name aligns with God's promise to Abraham by its meaning; "Father of a multitude".

## 5. What is represented by requiring Abraham and his descendent to be circumcised?

- It would identify those that were part of the promise to Abraham.
- It represented a complete enclosure of God's will.
- It was a sign of faith on the part those involved.
- It was a reminder to the man that every part of his body belonged to God.
- It was a sign of being set apart for God's purpose.

## 6. How can you use this lesson to grow spiritually and help others come into a relationship with Jesus?

We must submit to God's will, not ours. God is our creator and savior and knows what is best for us. Although we may not understand God's will in a situation, we know that it is in God's will that we are sanctified, live pure lives and love our brother (1 Thessalonians 4:1-11). Sanctified means being set aside. We are sanctified today through our baptism. The practice of circumcision was symbolic of our baptism today (Colossians 2:11 – an expression of faith).

As we submit to God's will, we express our humility as faithful servants to God. This clears the way for God to use our lives in ways beyond our limited imagination. We do not know God's timeline so we must develop the patience necessary to sustain our faith. We know God will act according to His will and His time.

# Lesson 32 – Lot's Poor Choices

## Teaching Strategy

The focus of this lesson is to review the consequences of Lot's choices concerning where he chose to live with his family after separating from Abraham. Of special note in this lesson is how we sometimes misuse the gift of free will and how God redirects us from where we are to where He wants us to be.

## Student Learning Outcomes

- **Know**: Realize the impact that our choices have on our relationship with God.

- **Feel**: Appreciate the importance of aligning our will with God's will.

- **Do**: Demonstrate faithfulness to God by seeking His will in all aspects of our lives.

## Support

- Series – Genesis – Foundational Book of the Bible (Mike Mazzalongo)

- Video – Lesson 32 – Lot's Poor Choices

- Student Note Guide for Lesson 32

## Body of the Lesson

1.1    The visit to Abraham
1.2    Lot at the gates of Sodom
1.3    Lessons

# Discussion Questions

Below are suggested questions to use during the guided discussion portion of the lesson. There are also suggested responses to questions to help students grasp the various concepts. These are provided to assist the discussion and are not considered as "right or wrong" responses.

## 1. Summarize the events of Genesis 18:1-20 and answer the following questions.

The purpose of this question is to ensure that students know the events leading to the destruction of Sodom and Gomorrah.

The Lord appears to Abraham in the form of a man, along with two angels who also appear in the form of men. Lot recognizes the significance of the men as the narrative indicates and later understood that he was speaking to God. Abraham invites them to refresh themselves with food and water. During this visit God lets Abraham know that Sarah will have a son in a year's time. Sarah was listening and laughs at the thought since she is now beyond the normal childbearing years. God then decides to tell Abraham of His plans to destroy Sodom and Gomorrah.

**What were the stated reasons for God's visit with Abraham?**

To let Abraham know that his son would be born in a year. To let him know of the upcoming destruction of Sodom and Gomorrah.

**What was Sarah's reaction when she heard about delivering a child and how does this relate to her previous attempt to provide an heir for Abraham through her servant, Hagar?**

Her reaction was to scoff at the idea since she was now well beyond normal child delivery years. This indicates that she still had a weak faith in God's promises and abilities.

**What were the reasons Sodom and Gomorrah were destroyed?**

They had become a wicked city rejecting God. Recall that Abraham had saved them from the northern Kings. Melchizedek and Lot lived righteously in their midst, yet even their example was not enough to change their sinful ways.

## 2. What is significant about Abraham's attempt to intercede for Sodom and Gomorrah?

It shows the merciful character of God.  In 2 Peter 3:9 we read, "The Lord is not slow to fulfill his promise as some count slowness, but is patient toward you, not wishing that any should perish, but that all should reach repentance."  God gives warnings all throughout scripture to those who have violated His will to turn back to Him.  His patience, however, has a limit and to exercise justice to the disobedient, He eventually punishes.  In this specific incident God revealed that the time for destruction was imminent but was willing to wait in order to honor Abraham's request to save Lot and his family.

We learn from this that we must not test the Lord's patience but be ready for His promised return and judgement (Matthew 25).  Our objective is to be found faithful when He comes.

## 3. What is significant about Lot sitting at the gates of Sodom?

Lot was active in the life of the city, thus well known.  Having been identified as a righteous man it is possible that he took advantage of this recognition to teach and be an example of righteousness.  Lot is approached there by the two angels (men) and invites them to his home for the night.

Lot made the conscious choice to live in Sodom.  Whether it was a wicked city at the time of his choosing, or became one later, Lot still had the choice to leave, but decided to remain there.  We, at times, find ourselves surrounded by evil no matter where we live.  We must, therefore, choose to remain faithful and if necessary move away to a safer situation in order to avoid temptation and guard our souls.

## 4. Discuss the mob's reaction to the visitors.

The mob in its depravity sought to rape the men. Lot refuses to turn them over, offering instead his daughters. The mob rejects this and attempts to take the men by force. The angels blind the mob and save Lot and his daughters from them.

## 5. Who was saved from the destruction of the city, who was not, and what is the significance of this?

Lot, his wife and daughters were saved from the destruction. All others were destroyed. Later, Lot's wife would perish when she looked back at the city's destruction. This indicates she did not have the faith to believe that God would act.

The significance of this is that Lot's sons-in-law rejected the protection offered by the Lord. Had they also gone, God would have spared the city (10 righteous). We must believe God at His word that He will return and destroy the wicked. We must not be among that number but be ready for His return. We must also do our best to influence others, especially our families in order to be found faithful.

**6. What is indicated regarding the faith of Lot's daughters from their actions in Genesis 9:30-38?**

The daughters do not have sufficient faith to understand that God saved them from destruction and would provide what they needed. They acted beyond God's will, just as Sarah had with her servant, Hagar. As a result, their offspring would be a problem for Israel through the Moabites and Ammonites. It is significant that Ruth, also a Moabite, would be in the lineage of Jesus. God has a way of turning lives around to His purpose, no matter who we are or our situation.

## 7. How can you use this lesson to grow spiritually and help others come into a relationship with Jesus?

There are many moving parts in these chapters. They all seem to revolve around faithfulness. We show our faithfulness to God as we live pure lives according to His will, and as we help others prepare for the eventual coming of our Lord.

It also shows that nothing is impossible with God (Luke 1:37; Matthew 19:26). This is true whether it is seen in destruction or salvation. God created us, loves us and desires above all else to save us. However, we are given the choice to accept or reject that love. We must pray that we always choose wisely.

God meets out mercy and justice. The mercy is in the form of the graceful offer of salvation. The justice is in the punishment of those who reject Him and the protection of those who accept Him.

Once we make the decision to follow our Lord then we must press forward and not look back. Hebrews 10:26-31 is a sober reminder of not returning to our former sinful lives. Just as Lot's wife was destroyed, so shall we be if we turn back to our sinful ways.

# Lesson 33 – The Source of Islam

## Teaching Strategy

The focus of this lesson is to understand the history of the people who would eventually embrace the Islamic religion. Of special note in this lesson is Abraham's continued walk of faith and how Islam began.

## Student Learning Outcomes

- **Know**: Understand how Abraham remained faithful through various challenges.

- **Feel**: Determine to grow in faith in spite of challenges we face.

- **Do**: Use the information gained from Genesis to strengthen our faith.

## Support

- Series – Genesis – Foundational Book of the Bible (Mike Mazzalongo)

- Video – Lesson 33 – The Source of Islam

- Student Note Guide for Lesson 33

## Body of the Lesson

1.1    Failure (20:1-18)
1.2    The child of promise
1.3    Lessons

# Discussion Questions

Below are suggested questions to use during the guided discussion portion of the lesson. There are also suggested responses to questions to help students grasp the various concepts. These are provided to assist the discussion and are not considered as "right or wrong" responses.

# 1. Summarize the events of Genesis 20:1-18 and answer the following questions.

The intent of this question is to ensure understanding of the events in this passage.

Abraham leaves for a trip into the land of the Philistines. He repeats the same sin as with the Egyptians where he lied about Sarah being his sister rather than his wife. As a result, the king takes Sarah into his harem. When he realizes the truth of Sarah's identity he releases her. Although he is angry with Abraham, he realizes that he is a prophet of God and furthermore enriches him.

**Why would Abraham repeat the lie he had told previously?**

Answers will vary but the desired response is that Abraham was still weak in his faith. Perhaps the greatest manifestation of this is impatience. Although God had provided multiple examples of His faithfulness to the covenant with Abraham, Abraham still had problems trusting God in difficult circumstances.

We are often this way as well. When we face the point of decision in difficult issues, we often try to take action on our own without realizing the promise that God will help us. We fail to seek God's wisdom through prayer. Acting on faith is expected of us, but we must always ensure that our prayers are in keeping with God's will and with consideration of His promise to respond to our prayers in His time and way.

**Although Abraham clearly lied, a violation of God's will, why would God enable him to gain further riches and rewards from this incident?**

Perhaps God was showing Abraham that despite his weakened faith, God still held the promise of making Abraham a great man. Abraham's admission of his lie may have been a form of repentance and led to a favorable outcome.

## 2. How was Isaac born and what was the significance of his birth?

Isaac was born in the same way children have always been born, except for the advanced age of Sarah. The significance of this is that it further demonstrates God's power over nature and His control of the timeline for fulfilling His covenant with Abraham.

## 3. Summarize the events leading to God's promise to Hagar from Genesis 20:9-20. Answer the following questions.

Isaac is weaned and Abraham celebrates this occasion with a feast. Sarah perceives that Hagar is mocking her so she has Hagar and Ismael driven from the camp. As Hagar and Ismael wander in the desert, her water runs dry so she sets Ismael aside to wait for him to die. God responds to her distress by promising that Ismael will become a great nation. God provided her with water thus saving their lives. They move on to Egypt where she raises Ismael.

**Discuss why Sarah would be jealous of Hagar since she was Abraham's wife and Isaac the heir.**

Human nature is strong. Sarah becomes jealous of the attention and position held by Hagar. Perhaps she sees her as a constant reminder of her own personal failure of faith.

**Why would God allow another nation to arise that would compete against His people?**

This is a challenging thought. Perhaps it was to strengthen Israel by having a constant challenge. It is also very possible that God recognized Hagar's faith through her prayers and saw this as a way to answer her. It may not have been God's intention for the descendants of Ismael to compete with Abraham's descendants. It is very likely that just as with many of us, Satan uses others to divide us and destroy our relationship with God.

## 4. Discuss how the reliance of legalistic works as seen in Islam and Judaism conflict with grace.

Expect various insights into this. The intent is for us to gain greater understanding of grace.

God implemented His laws and expects us to obey them. Grace has always been a part of God's plan, even within legalistic applications. It is seen by His willingness to forgive us and continue with us, even as we fail. This is seen in His faithfulness to Abraham and Sarah when they failed but returned to Him. It is seen in Hagar and Ismael as God recognized Hagar's plea and faith.

In our relationship with God we are asked to accept God's grace by acting upon our faith. God does not require a complete faith but does require us to grow in our faith. The more we grow the more we realize God's love and grace. This should spur us on to greater faithfulness.

## 5. How can you use this lesson to grow spiritually and help others come into a relationship with Jesus?

We never achieve perfect or complete faithfulness in this lifetime. This is not an excuse to give up, however, it is God's expectation that we learn to seek His will as we make decisions.

All too often we sin by taking matters into our own hands and try to impose our will or desires upon God rather that patiently waiting according to His will. As with Abraham and Sarah, even though they were in an advanced age and had seen God working throughout their lives, they still sinned.

We all face peaks and valleys in our journeys of faith. If we find ourselves in a valley, we should seek to determine what brought us there. If it was of our actions, then we pray for wisdom, correct our actions and bring them back into line with God's will. Sometimes we find ourselves in a valley for reasons beyond our control or as a result of another's poor decisions. In such circumstances we should still pray and ask God for wisdom to leave the valley. We should also pray for patience to bear under while in the valley and not just pray to leave.

A point of note, the richest soil is found in valleys. If we find ourselves in a valley, in addition to seeking a way out, look also for how we can glorify God and teach others of His greatness. In doing so we are working as God wills. Scripture is full of examples of God's people remaining faithful in the deepest of life's valleys. A great example is found in the book of Hebrews. The men and women mentioned here are faithful, "And all these, though commended through their faith, did not receive what was promised, since God had provided something better for us, that apart from us they should not be made perfect." (Hebrews 11:39-40 ESV). God has given us the fulfilled promise of hope and life through Jesus.

# Lesson 34 – Abraham's Test

### Teaching Strategy

The focus of this lesson is to review the events of God's instruction that Abraham sacrifice Isaac. Of special note in this lesson is the relationship between Abraham's test and God's deep love for us, and how testing strengthens our faith.

### Student Learning Outcomes

- **Know**: Compare Abraham's sacrifice of Isaac to God's sacrifice of Jesus.

- **Feel**: Recognize the depth of love God has for us.

- **Do**: Use the information gained from Genesis to strengthen our faith.

### Support

- Series – Genesis – Foundational Book of the Bible (Mike Mazzalongo)

- Video – Lesson 34 – Abraham's Test

- Student Note Guide for Lesson 34

### Body of the Lesson

1.1   Test of Faith
1.2   Lessons

## Discussion Questions

Below are suggested questions to use during the guided discussion portion of the lesson. There are also suggested responses to questions to help students grasp the various concepts. These are provided to assist the discussion and are not considered as "right or wrong" responses.

**1. Summarize the events of Abraham's test from Genesis 22 and answer the following questions.**

**How does God refer to Isaac when He addresses Abraham in Genesis 22:2, and what is significant about this?**

The intent of this question is to draw the clear imagery symbolized by this sacrifice as a type of God's sacrifice of Jesus.

God refers to Isaac as, "your son, your only son, whom you love." The significance of this is to communicate to Abraham then, and us today, the value of Isaac to Abraham. This son's importance to Abraham is intensified when we realize how long Abraham waited for Isaac to be born.

It further lays the foundation for understanding the relationship between God and Jesus, and the depth of love God has for us. Jesus was God's Son, His only Son and His beloved Son. This adds an incredible depth of understanding to John 3:16 and other references discussing God's willingness to sacrifice Jesus for our sins.

**How was Abraham's love for Isaac like God's love for us?**

The kind of love shown here is a father's love for his son. This is the same love God has for Jesus and His love for us as His children. A wonderful difference between Abraham's love for Isaac and God's love for us is that God loves us even before we accept Him, and even when we so frequently disobey Him. This is the love communicated in the parable of the Prodigal Son (Luke 15). This love is such that seeks only the best for the Prodigal even at the father's personal sacrifice and loss.

**How does the testing of Abraham and the testing of Job compare?**

In Job we see that God allowed Satan to test Job in order to show that Job's faith would fail if he lost all he had. Satan destroys all of Job's possessions and kills his children. Job's faith does not waiver even though he does not understand why God is allowing these evil events. In similar fashion God called upon Abraham to give up his most precious "possession", his deeply loved son, Isaac. Abraham demonstrated the strength of his faith, even though he did not understand the reason for God's demand.

God allows us to be tested. He does not personally bring the tests into our lives but allows them to happen. In doing so, as James states in James 1:2-4, when we withstand the demands of the test we see our faith grow stronger.

## 2. Explain how the faith Abraham shows by obeying God is the type of faith that God seeks from us.

The faith God wishes for us to develop is a deep, trusting faith that acts even if we don't understand. When we exhibit that level of faith then nothing will prevent us from obeying and serving God.

## 3. What are some reasons for testing as seen in scripture?

One use of testing is to determine one's faith as we see in the case of Abraham. Another use is to help us understand a concept. In the context of our spiritual relationship, Satan uses tests (temptations) to draw us into evil or to destroy our holy relationship with God. This serves to weaken our faith. This is behind the various temptations Satan used against Jesus (Matthew 4).

Test are also used to teach us. Abraham learned through this test. In John 6 Jesus "tests" Philip to teach him about Jesus' power and to offer a lesson on faith. James

1:2-4 tells us to rejoice in trials (tests) because they produce steadfastness and completeness. Abraham passed the test and had his faith strengthened.

We also face tests in our lives in various forms. When we stand fast in our faith, our faith grows. It is a positive cycle of spiritual growth. We also can learn from the tests of others, both through their failures and their victories which help strengthen our own faith.

## 4. List the various symbolic events in this test of Abraham and explain how they help us understand God's will.

This information is directly from the text for this lesson.

- The sacrifice of Christ
- Vicarious atonement
- Relationship between faith and works

## 5. How can you use this lesson to grow spiritually and help others come into a relationship with Jesus?

We must be aware that when we seek a relationship with God, Satan will seek to attack us in order to prevent that relationship (1 Peter 5:8-10). He does this in a variety of ways, one of which is to manipulate relationships that are valuable to us. We must also understand that Satan will continue to attack us by weakening relationships or destroying our effectiveness as a child of God. It is important, therefore, that we resolve to strengthen our faith and develop a greater reliance on God. We do this through various ways including: prayer, knowledge of God's word, relationships with fellow Christians and going on the offensive in our service to God (Ephesians 6:10-18).

# Lesson 35 – Types in Genesis

## Teaching Strategy

The focus of this lesson is a review of important types or previews within Genesis which are seen centuries later in the New Testament. Of special note in this lesson is Abraham in search of a bride for Isaac and how this previews the Church as the Bride of Christ.

## Student Learning Outcomes

- **Know**: Understand the type represented by Abraham and his search of a bride for Isaac to the Church as the Bride of Christ.

- **Feel**: Recognize the depth of desire God has to establish and maintain a relationship with us.

- **Do**: Use the information gained from Genesis to strengthen our faith.

## Support

- Series – Genesis – Foundational Book of the Bible (Mike Mazzalongo)

- Video – Lesson 35 – Types in Genesis

- Student Note Guide for Lesson 35

## Body of the Lesson

1.1    Abraham's search for a bride for Isaac
1.2    Types from Genesis
1.3    Lessons

# Discussion Questions

Below are suggested questions to use during the guided discussion portion of the lesson. There are also suggested responses to questions to help students grasp the various concepts. These are provided to assist the discussion and are not considered as "right or wrong" responses.

**1. Summarize the oath between Abraham and his messenger, and discuss the connection between the "hand under the thigh" and God's requirement of circumcision.**

The messenger was to not take a wife for Isaac from the Canaanites (pagans, and not God's people).  He was to go to Abraham's people.

The hand under the thigh represented a solemn agreement between the servant and Abraham but since it invoked God, it was also sacred oath.  Its connection to circumcision is that it was a covenant that was not to be broken.  It is also seen as an extension of the covenant between God and Abraham as this union between Isaac and his wife would produce the next generation of God's people.

**2. How can this activity also be a test of faith for those involved? What does this teach us?**

- **Abraham** – He was placing the outcome in God's hands working through the servant.

- **The Messenger** – He demonstrated great faith in accepting the challenge and placing the outcome in God's hands.  The servant prayed for God's guidance and revelation in the selection of a bride.

- **Rebekah** – She would demonstrate great faith in accepting the offer and leaving her home to start a life with Isaac.

As we seek to follow God's will, we too must pray for His guidance in making our choices.  Our prayers should include a desire for God's wisdom to make choices that reflect His will for our lives.  Sometimes the specific response from God is not seen in a direct way, but only realized through hindsight.  However, if we are seeking God's guidance as a priority component in making decisions, His will is going to be part of the outcome.  Abraham, now advanced in years, recognized the need for Isaac to marry.
He demonstrated a desire for God's will by ensuring that the wife would be from those whom God would approve and not from the pagan people in the area.

It would likely have been much simpler and quicker for the servant, but he refused to take the easy way.  Sometimes Satan tempts (tests) us by offering an easier way.  We must be careful to ensure that we are seeking and taking God's way, no matter what the cost.

## 3. What can we learn about following God's will from Rebekah's family?

Once they understood that it was God's will for Rebekah to become Isaac's wife, they enthusiastically approved the plan.  We should have the same attitude once we recognize God's will.  This is especially true in our initial response to obey the gospel but is just as true in our efforts to live faithfully each day.  God outlines what His will is.

For example, in 1 Thessalonians 4 Paul teaches us how to make our lives pleasing to God. He presents three elements: (1) Our salvation (sanctification); (2) pure living (represented by refraining from sexual immorality); (3) loving one another.

We can use these three standards to measure many of our daily decisions. Jesus taught this in Matthew 22:37-40 as He answered the apostles concerning the greatest commandment, "Love the Lord your God with all your heart, soul, and mind. And the second is like it, love your neighbor as yourself."  John echoed this in 1 John 3:23-24:  We believe in the name of Jesus, love one another as Jesus commands, Keep His commandments as we abide in God and in this way know that He abides in us through His Holy Spirit.

In short, we do not hesitate to fully obey God's will upon discovering it.

## 4. How is the messenger's actions a type of the Holy Spirit and the church?

See the associated text for further detail.

The messenger's work in bringing Rebekah to Isaac is like the action of the Holy Spirit bringing the Church to Christ as the bride of Christ. The Holy Spirit presents us gifts that enable us to serve faithfully. The Holy Spirit helps us grow spiritually in order to become more presentable as the Bride of Christ.

## 5. How are Isaac and Rebekah seen as a "type" for Christ and the Church?

See the associated text for this response.

## 6. How can you use this lesson to grow spiritually and help others come into a relationship with Jesus?

As a faithful servant of God we must seek and obey His will. In doing so we will be given entrance into God's eternal Kingdom. There are times when we might second guess our decisions as to whether we are in fact doing God's will, and sometimes we might deviate from it. However, we must strive to the best of our ability to entrust ourselves to God's care. He does not hide His will from us. When we find we have deviated from His will, we must quickly return to His way.

# Lesson 36 – The Life of Esau and Jacob

## Teaching Strategy

This lesson covers the transition from Isaac to his sons, Esau and Jacob. Of special note in this lesson is record of how Jacob became the heir rather than his brother Esau and the lessons from this to us.

## Student Learning Outcomes

- **Know**: Understand how God uses the choices we make to carry out His will.

- **Feel**: Value the importance of seeking and following God's will.

- **Do**: Use the information gained from Genesis to strengthen our faith.

## Support

- Series – Genesis – Foundational Book of the Bible (Mike Mazzalongo)

- Video – Lesson 36 – The Life of Esau and Jacob

- Student Note Guide for Lesson 36

## Body of the Lesson

1.1    The death of Abraham
1.2    Esau and Jacob
1.3    The birthright
1.4    Isaac vs. the Philistines
1.5    Lessons

# Discussion Questions

Below are suggested questions to use during the guided discussion portion of the lesson. There are also suggested responses to questions to help students grasp the various concepts. These are provided to assist the discussion and are not considered as "right or wrong" responses.

**1. How was the writer of Genesis able to describe Abraham's life as, "an old man and satisfied with life" or "full of years" (Genesis 25:7) and how can we achieve this in our lives?**

Abraham had many turns in his life. Parts of his life were mountain top experiences and others were lived in the deepest of valleys. As we look at the panorama of his life we see, however, that his focus was always in doing God's will. Sometimes, in the testing and development of his life, he strayed from God's will. Yet, he returned where God was able to redirect him towards the ultimate promise of greatness for himself and the people that would come after him.

We experience much of the same in our spiritual journey. It is never a straight upward trajectory, but rather an up and down, even backward experience at times. Yet, we continue to keep our eyes focused on the Lord and always return to doing His will. As 1 John 1:5-10 teaches us, God is faithful to forgive us and restore us to serving Him.

**2. Which phase or event in Abraham's life stands out most to you as one that you can identify with or learn the most from?**

Answers will certainly vary in this question. Look for examples of how even though Abraham seemed to be weak in his faith, he never-the-less strove to remain in God's will. Also look for examples that show God's grace towards Abraham especially during his periods of weakness.

**3. Discuss how Isaac, praying for his wife to conceive, demonstrates faith, and how this differs from Sarah's plan to resolve her inability to conceive.**

Rather than take action to produce children in a way different than what God willed, Isaac first relied on God to intervene. There is no indication that Rebekah, like Sarah, sought a way to produce an heir outside of the covenant relationship between herself and Isaac.

**4. Why would God choose Jacob to inherit the birthright of Isaac rather than Esau, the first born?**

There is no indicator in the narrative but God certainly knew the character of these men. This has been done before as God made choices based on character and not social expectations or outward appearances. Jacob would need testing and training to develop, but God knew the raw materials he possessed and how Jacob would eventually become the man God wanted him to be.

Our role is to develop the character God can use for His will. Even if we have been outside of God's will and characterized as self-serving, we can change. Through God's grace, our commitment to Him and our submission to the Holy Spirit, we can develop a character useful to God.

## 5. Review Genesis 26 and answer the following questions:

**Why did Isaac enter into an agreement with the King of the Philistines?**

A famine came upon the land and Isaac sought a solution rather than rely on God's providence.

**What was the result of Isaac living in Gerar?**

God forbade Isaac from entering Egypt. Isaac accepted God's direction. As a result God blesses Isaac with material wealth and stature in the land, even beyond that of the King to whom Isaac had turned for protection.

**What was the ultimate blessing provided by God to Isaac and why?**

God renewed the promise to Isaac that He had made to Abraham. He did this for the reasons stated in Genesis 26:5, "because Abraham obeyed Me and kept My charge, My commandments, My statues and My laws."

Note that this was because of Abraham's faithfulness and not Isaac's. Isaac was weak in faith at this point in his life. God, however, knew his heart and the potential Isaac had to become faithful.

**What can we learn from this?**

We are blessed by God in many ways. Certainly, we are blessed as we obey our Father, but we're also blessed in periods of unbelief. God does not destroy us when we sin. Rather, He patiently and lovingly disciplines us to bring us back to Him. This is His promise to us in 1 John 1:5-10.

## 6. How can you use this lesson to grow spiritually and help others come into a relationship with Jesus?

When God adds us to His kingdom, we become servants seeking to do the Master's will in all things.  Yet, the world continues to press in on us.  Satan attacks us to weaken our faith and destroy our effectiveness.  In times of weakness, we tend to give in or try to resolve the situation by our own wills and without regard to God's will working on our behalf.  We should first turn to God for wisdom, strength and courage with the intent of seeking and doing His will.

God recognizes our weaknesses and lovingly guides us home (Prodigal Son - Luke 15).  We must take steps to remain in God's will, and when not in His will, take steps to humbly return because the promise of salvation is always there for us.

# Lesson 37 – The Battle for Blessings

## Teaching Strategy

The focus of this lesson is the impact of Jacob's deceit in obtaining Esau's blessings and how God's will is completed despite the manipulations of men. Of special note in this lesson is the impact of Rebekah and Jacob's plot and how God's will was still accomplished.

## Student Learning Outcomes

- **Know**: Understand how God continues to demonstrate His love and grace despite the manipulations of men.

- **Feel**: Appreciate God's continued love and grace even during our times of weakness.

- **Do**: Use the information gained from Genesis to strengthen our faith.

## Support

- Series – Genesis – Foundational Book of the Bible (Mike Mazzalongo)

- Video – Lesson 37 – The Battle for Blessings

- Student Note Guide for Lesson 37

## Body of the Lesson

1.1     The deception
1.2     The impact of the deception
1.2     Lessons

# Discussion Questions

Below are suggested questions to use during the guided discussion portion of the lesson. There are also suggested responses to questions to help students grasp the various concepts. These are provided to assist the discussion and are not considered as "right or wrong" responses.

## 1. Summarize Genesis 27:1-46 how Rebekah and Jacob deceived Isaac and answer the following questions.

The intent of this question is to learn how God's will remains and will be met. Sometimes, as seen in this situation as well as previous actions by Sarah and Abraham, we try to take shortcuts or circumvent God's will. God continues to work His will despite human interference.

### Why would God not punish Rebekah and Jacob for their deception?

Although the plan was not according to God's will, the outcome still met with His overall purpose. It is possible that God let His covenant hold greater weight than the need for immediate retribution. In truth, Jacob did struggle as a result of his deception. Just as God controls time for answering prayer and fulfilling His promises, He controls when and how He punishes.

### How does God's choice of when and how to punish relate to Matthew 24:36 regarding the return of our Lord?

Only God knows the when and how. Our role is to be faithful and ready for a date known only to God. His will is fulfilled as He desires and when He does so.
As seen in the outcome of the deceit of Rebekah and Jacob, God's will was fulfilled in Jacob receiving the birthright and superiority over his brother.

## 2. Read Genesis 27:34-47 and answer the following questions.

### What was the immediate outcome once Esau realized Jacob had cheated him of his birthright?

Esau became extremely saddened and angry.  As a result of this deceit, the family was torn apart and would remain so for years.  Furthermore, the natural way of the oldest receiving the birthright and prominence in the family was reversed.

### What was Esau's plan once he realized his mother and brother's deceived?

Esau plotted to murder his brother.  Hate is intense loathing or passionate dislike for someone.  If not controlled or eliminated, it results in irrational and violent behavior.

Esau had every right and expectation to become angry because of the deceit (Regardless of the fact that in his weakness he brought it on himself).  In his hatred and anger he developed murderous intent.  This was both a heart and attitude issue.

### How does Esau's plan for revenge on his brother relate to Jesus' teachings on hate and murder (Matthew 5:21), 1 John 3:15, and Ephesians 4:26-27?

In Matthew 5:21, Jesus considered it murder to sink to this depth of hatred and anger. In 1 John 3:15, John echoes this and warns again that if we do not abide in love, we do not have eternal life.  Paul not only warns about anger but tells us to make haste in resolving our anger so that Satan does not gain a foothold in our hearts.
Paul concludes this passage with the admonition to be kind to one another, tenderhearted, forgiving one another as God in Christ forgave us.  Esau was wronged by Rebekah and Jacob, but he was not without fault in this series of events.

### 3. How does this event point to God's grace?

God made a promise to Abraham to make him a great name and a great nation. God was bound by His love and grace to keep that covenant. Even though His offspring were not faithful at times, God still remembered the promise. Furthermore, God will not remove free will as part of man's godlike character. He will deal with the consequences of poor choices and offer us better choices and opportunities to renew our decisions.

As always happens with our failures, we learn that God's grace is boundless. Tied to God's grace is His unfathomable love. From Adam and Eve to now, God takes us as we are and where we are, and gently leads us to where He wants us to be.

God also knows the outcome of our lives because of His omniscience. He knew the heart of Jacob and what Jacob could become. Our view is all too often short-sighted, unlike God Who has an eternal view.

### 4. How can you use this lesson to grow spiritually and help others come into a relationship with Jesus?

It is sometimes difficult to see how God is working in our lives. We experience our wants and needs and desire immediate resolutions. The challenge is to achieve the proper balance between acting and acting according to God's will. This requires continual prayer for wisdom and patience. God has promised to be with us. This does not mean that we will never face adverse situations. It does, however, mean that we will not face them alone. God gives us comfort through His word, our brothers and sisters in the Lord, and the Holy Spirit. We need to remember this as we deal with life's valleys. Sometimes we don't see God working with us through difficult times until we're through the valley, but we can rely on His promises none-the-less.

# Lesson 38 – Jacob's Family

## Teaching Strategy

The focus of this lesson is to learn how Jacob began to carry out God's covenant made with Abraham. Of special note in this lesson is the renewal of the covenant with Jacob and Jacob's initial actions.

## Student Learning Outcomes

- **Know**: Understand how God continues to demonstrate His faithfulness to the covenant made with Abraham.

- **Feel**: Recognize how God uses imperfect vessels to achieve His will.

- **Do**: Use the information gained from Genesis to strengthen our faith.

## Support

- Series – Genesis – Foundational Book of the Bible (Mike Mazzalongo)

- Video – Lesson 38 – Jacob's Family

- Student Note Guide for Lesson 38

## Body of the Lesson

1.1    The blessing
1.2    Esau's reaction
1.3    Jacob's ladder
1.4    Jacob and Laban
1.5    Jacob's sons
1.6    Lessons

# Discussion Questions

Below are suggested questions to use during the guided discussion portion of the lesson. There are also suggested responses to questions to help students grasp the various concepts. These are provided to assist the discussion and are not considered as "right or wrong" responses.

# 1. What is significant about Isaac redoing the blessing upon Jacob?

Even though Jacob obtained the birthright by deception, Isaac recognized it was God's will that Jacob receive the blessing and later the covenant with God. This is despite Jacob taking actions contrary to how God would have brought this about.

# 2. What was significant about Esau's reaction to Isaac blessing Jacob?

It was with a sense of finality that Esau realized his brother would receive the birthright and blessing. There seems to be a level of repentance involved as well. He marries more in line with what Isaac wanted rather than taking another pagan wife.

# 3. What is represented by the ladder in Jacob's dream (Genesis 28:12; John 1:51) and what is the significance of this to us?

The ladder was the link between heaven and earth symbolizing movement (spiritual as well as physical). As part of their role, angels minister to those that are God's people through and on behalf of Jesus.

# 4. Summarize the events in Genesis 28 that speak to the covenant of God with Jacob and how we can apply this to our lives?

Verse 4 – Abraham's blessing is transferred so Jacob could take possession of the land.
Verse 13 – God gives Jacob the land.
Verse 14 – God promises that Jacob's offspring will be countless, just as He had promised Abraham.
Verse 15 – God promises to be with Jacob and would bring him back to the land when he leaves.
All of this demonstrates the faithfulness of God to the promised made long before. God is also faithful to the promise He makes to us.

**5. Read the covenant God made with Jacob from Genesis 28:13-15 and answer the following questions.**

**What is significant about God not putting conditions on Jacob regarding the covenant and why is this significant for us?**

God takes us as we are and graciously, lovingly and patiently takes us to where He wants us to go. Jacob had a lot to learn and grow into, but he was beginning to turn towards God as evidenced by his obedience to his father and his reaction to God.

In like manner, when we turn to God, He guides us from where we are as imperfect people weak in our faith, to where He wants us to be more like Christ. He only asks us to be faithful, and when we fail, to repent and return to Him.

**How is God's promise to Jacob in verse 15 and 1 John 1:5-10 related to our relationship with God today?**

God made a promise to Jacob that He would be with him. In other words, He would sustain his relationship with Jacob, even when Jacob was weak. In like manner, God maintains His relationship with us, even during our weaknesses. God also promised Jacob that He would bring him back to the land. We know from the biblical account that Jacob did leave the land and settled in Egypt due to the famine, and at the invitation of Joseph. Then, following his death, Joseph returned Jacob's body to his homeland for burial (Genesis 49 and 50). Part of the providence of God regarding the life of Joseph included the fulfillment of the promise to Jacob to bring him home.

There are times when we stray from God's will by to our sin. Yet God is still with us as His faithful children. He takes us back into a relationship with Him as we confess our sins and repent. This is His promise to us. He will be with us and bring us home. That is His promise. Praise God for His love and faithfulness!

## 6. Summarize the events between Jacob and Laban from Genesis 29.

The intent of this question is to witness God's guidance in the difficult relationship Jacob had with Laban.

Jacob travels to the land of his ancestors in obedience to Isaac. There he meets Rachel. He enters into an agreement with Laban to labor for seven years to obtain Rachel as his wife. After the seven years Laban deceives Jacob by giving him his other daughter, Leah, instead. This results in seven more years of service in order to have Rachel as wife.

This event can be seen as punishment for Jacob's deceit in obtaining the birthright. As a minimum, the labor and anguish he endured in his service to Laban in order to marry Rachel can be seen as consequences for the deception of his brother and father.

During this time Jacob has 12 sons between Leah, Rachel and their maids. Although this was a form of polygamy God permitted it during this period of history. It later caused problems for the family. Certainly, anytime we go against God's will it results in difficulties and consequences.

## 7. How can you use this lesson to grow spiritually and help others come into a relationship with Jesus?

God makes a promise to us that we will be saved and added to His Kingdom when we believe in Jesus. This faith is expressed in repentance and baptism (Acts 2:38).

After this, God guarantees salvation so long as we remain faithful and continue to acknowledge our sins to Him (1 John 1:7-9).

# Lesson 39 – Jacob Leaves Laban

### Teaching Strategy

The focus of this lesson is to review Jacob's actions as he departs from Laban. Of special note in this lesson is Jacob and Laban's arrangement, Jacob's departure and lessons we can apply from these events.

### Student Learning Outcomes

- **Know**: Understand how God demonstrates His faithfulness to the initial promise to bring a Messiah, and His continued faithfulness to the covenant with Abraham.

- **Feel**: Develop an appreciation for how God uses existing situations to continue His covenant with man.

- **Do**: Use the information gained from Genesis to strengthen our faith.

### Support

- Series – Genesis – Foundational Book of the Bible (Mike Mazzalongo)

- Video – Lesson 39 – Jacob Leaves Laban

- Student Note Guide for Lesson 39

### Body of the Lesson

1.1     Jacob and Laban's arrangement
1.2     Jacob's departure
1.3     Lessons

## Discussion Questions

Below are suggested questions to use during the guided discussion portion of the lesson. There are also suggested responses to questions to help students grasp the various concepts. These are provided to assist the discussion and are not considered as "right or wrong" responses.

# 1. Summarize Genesis 30:24-43 and answer the following questions.

The intent of this question is to establish a foundation for understanding how God takes us where we are and continues to move us to become what He intends for us to be when we turn our lives over to Him.

### Why was Jacob a part of Laban's household?

Jacob had run away to avoid conflict from Esau following his deception in obtaining his father, Isaac's, blessing. He enters into an agreement with his kinsman, Laban, to work for 7 years to gain Rachel as his wife. Later, after being deceived by Laban, he agrees to work another 7 years for Rachel and 6 more years for the animals.

### How was Jacob blessed while a part of Laban's household?

This question can be answered two ways; spiritually and physically.

Spiritually, God blessed him by preserving his life and providing him with a better quality of life.

Physically, God gave him several sons by Leah and Rachel and their maids. He also prospered with his herds multiplying and gaining other physical possessions so that he was wealthier than Laban.

### What practical lesson can we learn about Jacob's work in service to Laban as it applies to our service for the Lord?

Jacob's hard work and persistence were rewarded. In like fashion, we must work hard and be persistent in our service to God. In Matthew 25 Jesus tells the parable of the talents. This parable is a glimpse into the judgment scene. In this parable, the master rewards the two servants for their hard work and faithfulness. The statement made to them is, "Well done, good and faithful servant." The unfaithful and slothful servant was punished and removed from the presence of the master.

## 2. Summarize the events of Genesis 31 and answer the following questions.

The intent of this question is to see how God orchestrates events to enable His will to be brought about. Sometimes God intervened directly but more times than not, He used the events happening to shape the outcome according to His will.

**Why does Jacob want to leave Laban if he's been successful as a part of his household?**

Jacob was told by the Lord to return to the land of his father and relatives. God also makes the promise that He will be with him. Perhaps Jacob has gone through a time of testing and growing so that he was now ready to follow God's will (Genesis 30:4-16).

**What was Laban's reaction to Jacob's departure and how was he thwarted in his attempt to stop Jacob?**

He was angry and sought to bring Jacob and his possessions back under his control. He was not successful due in part to God's warning not to act against Jacob. He does challenge Jacob but leaves without any of Jacob's family or possessions.

**If you wish to share, how has God used events in your life to bring about your faithful service to Him?**

The intent of this question is for us to reinforce in our own understanding how God directs our lives as we serve Him. It will also serve to reinforce in other's minds that God does work in our lives and will work in theirs as they learn to turn over more of their lives to Him. For this to happen, we must all learn to grow spiritually.

### 3. How can you use this lesson to grow spiritually and help others come into a relationship with Jesus?

We must learn to put our lives into God's hands. We know intellectually that we must do this but it is a lesson that takes a long time to master. As we grow spiritually, we find that we are able to do so and as a result, grow spiritually in practice.

We must also seek to not let sin find its way back into our lives. This requires an ongoing effort at being on guard against Satan's efforts against us (Ephesians 6:10-18; 1 Peter 5:8-9).

We, however, continue to serve faithfully knowing that our task is to serve our Lord, sow the seed of His word and always be ready to teach others the good news of Jesus Christ (2 Timothy 4:2).

# Lesson 40 – Jacob and Esau – Round 2

## Teaching Strategy

The focus of this lesson is to review the reconciliation between Jacob and Esau. Of special note in this lesson is the continued faithfulness of God to His initial promise to Abraham carried on through to Jacob.

## Student Learning Outcomes

- **Know**: Understand how God demonstrates His faithfulness to His initial promise of sending a Messiah and the continued faithfulness to the covenant with Abraham.

- **Feel**: Develop an appreciation for how God uses existing situations to continue His covenant with His chosen people.

- **Do**: Use the information gained from Genesis to strengthen our faith.

## Support

- Series – Genesis – Foundational Book of the Bible (Mike Mazzalongo)

- Video – Lesson 40 – Jacob and Esau - Round 2

- Student Note Guide for Lesson 40

## Body of the Lesson

1.1    God's protection revealed
1.2    Jacob prepares to meet Esau
1.3    Jacob wrestles with God
1.4    Jacob's meeting with Esau
1.5    Lessons

# Discussion Questions

Below are suggested questions to use during the guided discussion portion of the lesson. There are also suggested responses to questions to help students grasp the various concepts. These are provided to assist the discussion and are not considered as "right or wrong" responses.

# 1. Summarize Genesis 32:1-2 and discuss its significance.

The intent of this question is to show that God provides us with the necessary resources to meet the opportunities He places before us. It also demonstrates God's faithfulness to His promise.

Jacob has left Laban and is returning to his home as God directed. He does so with misgivings as to what to expect from Esau. He fears that Esau will still be seeking to harm him. God sends two angels to Jacob to demonstrate that he is not alone and that God is with him, as promised.

# 2. Why did Jacob send his servants before him to meet Esau?

There are several practical reasons. It was an expression of humility showing he did not need or desire Esau's possession and therefore was not a threat to his brother. Jacob still felt concern for his safety even though God reminded him of His promise of protection. Jacob was taking a practical approach to the reunion. Jacob was demonstrating that his success was from God and used for God's purposes. Jacob was also expressing, in his own way, his gratitude for God's graciousness.

**Note**: God uses us best when we work from our weaknesses. Paul recognized this and shared several times how God workd through his weaknesses. For example, 2 Corinthians 11:30, "If I must boast, I will boast of the things that show my weakness." and 2 Corinthians 12:9, "But he said to me, "My grace is sufficient for you, for my power is made perfect in weakness." (ESV)

## 3. Summarize Genesis 30:24-32 and answer the following questions:

### What is the context of Jacob's wrestling with God?

Jacob sent his servants and flocks ahead to meet Esau. He now is by himself to deal with his fears, doubts and prayers. The idea of being by himself communicates that he is perhaps "wrestling" with himself to come to a resolution to meet Esau. He is also questioning if he is doing the right thing. God appears to him in the form of a man and begins to struggle with Jacob. The struggle lasts through the night symbolizing a long and arduous experience. Jacob recognizes that he's struggling with God. The struggle then becomes an effort at clinging to God until he has assurances that God is with him (vs. 27). God then changes Jacob's name to "Israel" to symbolize his success.

### How was Jacob able to see God, "face to face" (vs. 30)?

The expression face to face means he recognized God. It was not a literal seeing God's face. Jacob clung to God until he was sure God would help him. Jacob's comments to God shows that he recognized that it was God he was dealing with, in the form of a man and not the actual form of God. It is similar to what happened with Abraham in Genesis 18.

### How do we see God "face to face"?

We face God when we open our hearts to Him and are made aware of and convicted of our shortcomings as God's Spirit works in our lives. We see God in the faithfulness of others. We see God as we recognize that we are growing in spiritual maturity as we turn our lives over to Him and see the Lord working through us.

## 4. Summarize the meeting between Jacob and Esau from Genesis 33:1-20 and discuss its significance to us.

Jacob finally meets Esau face to face. He separates his family and goes on ahead of them. He goes through an elaborate ritual of bowing before Esau showing total servitude. As a result, Esau runs to greet his brother to accept and forgive him. Esau has made the journey from hyper-jealousy and murderous intent to complete forgiveness.

It is obvious that God has softened the heart of Esau. This was God's way of demonstrating His faithfulness to the promise that He would protect Jacob. Even Esau recognized God's work by expressing how God had blessed him and that he did not need the gifts from Jacob.

We all have fears in our lives. We do and should seek God's protection and blessings with those fears. God promised to be there for us. We don't know how or when but we must develop the faith that He will provide. God not only answers our prayers, He answers them for our good and beyond our expectations.

## 5. How can you use this lesson to grow spiritually and help others come into a relationship with Jesus?

Years later Paul expresses a level of confidence that we too can feel. He states in Romans 8:31, "What then shall we say to these things? If God is for us, who can be against us?" (ESV)

We know that we should pray with the expectation that God will provide. This is a life-long lesson made more possible as our prayer lives grow and we see God working in our lives.

God works best when we turn ourselves over to Him in humility and weakness. We must get ourselves out of the way. This too takes a lifetime of learning.

# Lesson 41 – On the Run Again

## Teaching Strategy

The focus of this lesson is to review an episode in Jacob's life as he interacts with the pagan residents of the region. Of special note in this lesson are the consequences of deviating from God's will and God's continued faithfulness to His promise.

## Student Learning Outcomes

- **Know**: Understand how God brought about a renewal in the life of Jacob and his family and what we can learn from this for our own lives.

- **Feel**: Appreciate the importance of striving to follow God's will in all areas of our lives.

- **Do**: Seek to discover and find God's will as we strive for faithfulness.

## Support

- Series – Genesis – Foundational Book of the Bible (Mike Mazzalongo)

- Video – Lesson 41 – On the Run Again

- Student Note Guide for Lesson 41

## Body of the Lesson

1.1     The rape of Dinah
1.2     Jacob's renewal
1.3     Lessons

# Discussion Questions

Below are suggested questions to use during the guided discussion portion of the lesson. There are also suggested responses to questions to help students grasp the various concepts. These are provided to assist the discussion and are not considered as "right or wrong" responses.

# 1. Summarize the events of Genesis 34:1 – 36:43.

The intent of this question is to embed in the minds of the students how life in the time of Jacob had unique challenges to faithfulness and how weaknesses have consequences. During this period Jacob had settled back in the region of Canaan as God directed him. His family continued to grow and prosper. As the narrative begins, Jacob's daughter Dinah is raped by Shechem, the son of one of the kings in the region. Shechem then requests that his father arrange a marriage to Dinah. The king, Hamor, approaches Jacob to arrange the marriage that would result in an intermingling of the two peoples. Jacob's sons state that before they will consent, the men of Hamor's people must be circumcised. They did this as part of their plan for revenge. Hamor's men agree and follow-through. When they were healing from the circumcision, Jacob's sons killed Hamor and his son Shechem. Jacob recognizes the danger of what they did.

God speaks to Jacob and tells him to move to Bethel to live and to erect an altar to Him there. Part of this was to cleanse the people of pagan gods that had begun to be worshipped by some of the Israelites. Upon doing so, God renewed His promise with Jacob.

# 2. What concerns do we share with Jacob as we raise our families in a society that does not honor God?

We must take special care to raise our children in the knowledgeable of God and know what God requires of His people. Certainly, it is our goal to teach our children salvation, but we must also teach them the importance of faithfulness to God as well. Jacob had a level of faithfulness but at times exhibited weaknesses. One area he could have improved which serves as a direct lesson for us is the importance of being a spiritual leader of our homes.

Paul speaks to this in two of his letters. In Ephesians 5:25-33 and Colossians 3:18-25, Paul teaches that husbands are the head of the household. This is especially true in regards to spiritual leadership. In chapter 6 he adds a charge for fathers to teach their children faithfulness to the Lord. In situations where a family may not have a father, this falls to the mothers, but initially, as per God's plan, it is a direct responsibility of fathers and cannot be abdicated to someone else.

### 3. How did God renew His promise to Jacob (Genesis 35) and what can we learn from this?

God required Jacob to move out of the region where he was. This was not only a practical action given the dangers and complications that resulted from the actions against Hamor and his people, but it symbolized a fresh start. Jacob erected an alter to God reminding him of when he fled from Esau and God rescued him. God also required Jacob to purge from his family any false gods, to purify themselves and to change their garments. This represented a physical, spiritual and emotional cleansing.

It is easy for us to become complacent in our journey of faithfulness. We allow unnoticed things and attitudes to creep into our lives that interfer with our faithfulness. We must be on guard against these. However, when we recognize that we've deviated from God's will then we must be willing to "re-erect our altar to God" by renewing our faithfulness, purifying our lives and purging everything that interferes with our faithful service to God. It is a difficult task that may require drastic actions such as Jacob took, however, it is vital for our continued faithfulness and salvation.

## 4. How can you use this lesson to grow spiritually and help others come into a relationship with Jesus?

We must remember that relationships can affect our faithfulness to God. We're encouraged to create our families from among fellow believers so that we encourage and strengthen each other. We should foster that perspective in our children by encouraging them to associate with children of like faith so that as they grow up and select mates to begin their own families, they will also have a greater opportunity to select faithful Christian partners.

If we do not lead our families in faithfulness, then it is not likely to occur. As noted, this is a specific responsibility of fathers, but not fathers alone. Each of us must seek to "spur one another on to good works" (Hebrews 10:24). We can do this by encouraging our children to seek out Christian friends and mates.

When we recognize we've strayed from God, we must be willing to take whatever action is required to change our spiritual, physical and emotional situations to bring them back into alignment with God's will. We should also be willing to support others that are trying to do this as well.

# Lesson 42 – The Beginning of the End

## Teaching Strategy

The focus of this lesson is to review the beginning of the story of Joseph. Of special note in this lesson is how Joseph came to his position in Egypt and the role it played in God's eternal plan to bring Jesus to complete His work of redemption.

## Student Learning Outcomes

- **Know**: Understand how God uses the affairs of men to continue His promise of redemption.

- **Feel**: Develop an awareness of the role Genesis plays in God's overall plan for man.

- **Do**: Use the information gained from Genesis to strengthen our faith.

## Support

- Series – Genesis – Foundational Book of the Bible (Mike Mazzalongo)

- Video – Lesson 42 – The Beginning of the End

- Student Note Guide for Lesson 42

## Body of the Lesson

1.1    A new writer
1.2    Joseph and his dreams
1.3    Joseph sold into slavery
1.4    Lessons

# Discussion Questions

Below are suggested questions to use during the guided discussion portion of the lesson. There are also suggested responses to questions to help students grasp the various concepts. These are provided to assist the discussion and are not considered as "right or wrong" responses.

## 1. Summarize the evidence of a new writer for the Geneses narrative and the significance of this.

As the chapter begins, we see the end of the narrative of Jacob's life and the appearance of a new writer. The evidence is the telling of the dreams of Joseph. It seems logical that Joseph would be the one telling of the dreams and other details of the events that followed in his life.

There may be many reasons why this is significant but of major note is the turning of a page in the narrative of God's faithfulness to His covenant. It will now shift to Joseph as a key player in the fulfillment of the covenant. Note also that Jacob is living in the land of his father as a sojourner. Sojourner means traveler indicating that it is a transient life.

## 2. Summarize the dreams of Joseph from Genesis 37:2-11 and their impact on his relationship with his brothers.

Joseph dreams two dreams indicating that his family will one day serve him. The brothers become jealous and angry and sell him into slavery. This resulted in the chain of events that eventually led the Israelites receiving the Law of Moses and later on, the arrival of Jesus.

## 3. What is the relationship between Joseph's brothers selling him into slavery and our slavery into the bondage of sin?

Joseph's physical slavery and removal from his father is symbolic of our slavery to sin and how this results in the separation from our heavenly Father. Joseph did not choose separation, it was forced upon him by the actions of others. In our slavery, we may not always choose to sin, but throughout history the results of sin are none-the-less forced upon us. As a result, like Joseph we are separated from God. Joseph was physically removed as far as possible from his father. In the same way, our slavery to sin completely removes us from our Father. The blood of an innocent animal was shed in the transaction for Joseph. The innocent blood of Jesus was shed but not to separate us from the Father, but to reunite us.

## 4. What can we learn about our heavenly Father's grief at the separation we cause and the grief Jacob experienced when he was separated from Joseph?

Jacob experienced deep grief with seemingly no hope of ever seeing Joseph again. It is likely that he felt, as would any father, that he would rather have been taken than his son. In like fashion, our separation from God causes Him grief. He did in fact offer a part of Himself to die in our place through His Son, Jesus. This illustrates how deep the love of God is for us.

## 5. How can you use this lesson to grow spiritually and help others come into a relationship with Jesus?

God grants us wonderful gifts that we must use for His glory as He intends for us. God granted Joseph insights into His will for him. Joseph misinterpreted God's intent. As a result, he suffered the consequences. We see this today when we use our gifts from God, both physical and spiritual, for our own purposes and not God's.

No matter the gifts or our use of them, we need to continually refine our ability for ministry by study, prayer and practice. We should seek every opportunity to exercise our gifts to God's glory.

As we live according to God's will, Satan will interfere in order to shift our focus away from faithfulness. He will use our weaknesses and attempt to turn our strengths into weakness. We must be on guard for this and take an uncompromising stand for what is right. Joseph was a good example of this. As we review the life of Joseph we see that his faith in God and desire to live faithfully did not waiver.

# Lesson 43 – Judah and Tamar

### Teaching Strategy

The focus of this lesson is on the relationship of Judah and Tamar. Of special note in this lesson is the significant impact parents have on the faithfulness of children.

### Student Learning Outcomes

- **Know**: Understand the role and impact of our influence on family faithfulness.
- **Feel**: Value our role as spiritual leaders in our family.
- **Do**: Live as God would have us so as to be an effective role model.

### Support

- Series – Genesis – Foundational Book of the Bible (Mike Mazzalongo)
- Video – Lesson 43 – Judah and Tamar
- Student Note Guide for Lesson

### Body of the Lesson

1.1 The story of Judah
1.2 Lessons learned

## Discussion Questions

Below are suggested questions to use during the guided discussion portion of the lesson. There are also suggested responses to questions to help students grasp the various concepts. These are provided to assist the discussion and are not considered as "right or wrong" responses.

## 1. Summarize the key events of Genesis 38:10-30 and state their significance.

The intent of this question is to understand that we influence positively and negatively the faithfulness of our families and others. As students answer this look for elements of positive and negative actions that influence the spiritual faithfulness of Judah, Tamar and others. Also note that even with their weaknesses, God chose to continue His faithfulness through the lineage of those involved. God does not tolerate unfaithfulness but does continue to work His will through us despite our unfaithfulness at times. He takes a long view and offers grace despite our mistakes and weaknesses.

## 2. How do the events of Judah and Tamar's lives support the role of parents in influencing the faith of children?

(See also Ephesians 5:22-33; 6:1-4)

God has entrusted the rearing and teaching of children specifically to parents. This has always been His plan. Each parent has unique gifts and abilities to do so in unique ways with the ultimate purpose of guiding and guarding their souls. We cannot abdicate this to others nor ignore our responsibilities without dire consequences both in this life and for eternity.

### 3. How can parents recover their role as spiritual leaders of their families?

There is no absolute solution to recovering our influence once it's weakened or lost. We must make the effort, however. We can begin by making a personal commitment to bring our own lives into line with God's will. From there, by example and direct actions we begin to consistently practice God's will. Whether we directly teach or enlist the help of others (and perhaps we should involve others), we can begin to share God's word with our children. With younger children we can perhaps bring this about more easily. This underscores the importance of beginning early and maintaining our efforts. With older or adult children, we can speak with them and share our desire to renew our relationship with God and encourage them to do the same.

### 4. How can we influence an unbelieving partner to establish a relationship with God?

Seek input from those willing to share personal perspectives on this.

This is a very difficult thing to do but should be done none-the-less. Constant prayer, consistent example, patience and love are all part of the effort to establish an environment where conversion or repentance can occur. Don't give up. Believe that you are influencing for good. God works on our hearts to soften them but sometimes this process takes time.

## 5. What does the use of the four women mentioned in this event teach us about how God uses us?

God knows the unique abilities and opportunities we have. He doesn't force our compliance but always uses us as we seek opportunities to serve. The four women mentioned in this series of events show that God can and will use anyone, no matter their previous life situation if they will allow it. God has an eternal view and no action by man or Satan can defeat it. A person may be lost, but God's plan continues. These four women show how a person can be influenced for good. God takes us as we are and brings us to where he wants us to be.

## 6. How can you use this lesson to grow spiritually and help others come into a relationship with Jesus?

We see in this series of events and many others in scripture how God continues in His faithfulness. This should be an encouragement for us to do the same. When we live as God intends then our influence results in good for everyone involved. More to the point, it results in spiritual growth as we continue to be steadfast (James 1:2-4).

# Lesson 44 – Joseph's Story

### Teaching Strategy

The focus of this lesson is a review of Joseph's life in Potiphar's household and the events leading to his unjust imprisonment.  Of special note in this lesson is God's recognition and reward of Joseph's faithfulness and how this is an example for us.

### Student Learning Outcomes

- **Know**:  Summarize how God influences events to bring about His will.

- **Feel**:  Recognize the providence of God through events in our lives.

- **Do**:  Remain faithful to God no matter the circumstances of our lives.

### Support

- Series – Genesis – Foundational Book of the Bible (Mike Mazzalongo)

- Video – Lesson 44 – Joseph's Story

- Student Note Guide for Lesson 44

### Body of the Lesson

1.1    Ancient Egypt
1.2    Joseph at Potiphar's house
1.3    Joseph in prison
1.4    Lessons

## Discussion Questions

Below are suggested questions to use during the guided discussion portion of the lesson. There are also suggested responses to questions to help students grasp the various concepts. These are provided to assist the discussion and are not considered as "right or wrong" responses.

## 1. Discuss how the environment of ancient Egypt enabled Joseph to fulfill God's will.

The use of skilled labor to care for the day to day events of a household and for the building and maintenance of society proved a fertile ground for Joseph to demonstrate his God-given talents. This environment in general shows God's providence but still required Joseph's willingness to serve God.

All too often we don't see God's providence in our lives until much later. We should try to look for God's influence in our day to day activities. This will serve to strengthen our faith.

## 2. Summarize how Joseph came to be the steward of Potiphar's household with emphasis on Joseph's response to various events.

Through God's divine purpose, Joseph was gifted with the abilities to effectively run Potiphar's household. Potiphar's wife is attracted to him and desires to have a sexual relationship with him. Joseph refuses both for the sin involved. He is falsely accused by her of rape and winds up in prison.

Joseph demonstrates faithfulness, not only to his role as Potiphar's servant, but more so, as a servant of God. As a result, God continues to show favor upon Joseph, even in prison. The jailer recognizes Joseph's skills and places him in a favored position.

### 3. Summarize Joseph's time in prison and answer the following questions.

The intent of this question is to show how God's providence continues even in difficult times.

**Why would God not release Joseph from jail immediately?**

There could be many reasons why God did not release Joseph immediately. For example, perhaps God wished to bring all the elements together to create the perfect environment for Joseph to bring about God's will. Additionally, we should remember as Paul teaches us in 2 Corinthians 12:1-10 that God works best through our weaknesses. God was able to demonstrate it was His power and not Joseph's that brought about the events of Joseph's rise to his position in Pharaoh's court.

**How can we use Joseph's example to continue to serve God in times of trial?**

All of us go through periods of trial, some extreme while some are simply daily challenges. Regardless of the depth and scope, Joseph teaches us about faithfulness. He praised God in both good and hard times. We can look for opportunities to serve God in all situations. This is not easy, but with God's help, we can continue to serve Him. We must also recognize that God does not abandon us, especially in our times of weakness and helplessness.

**What can we do if we fail in our faithfulness during a hard situation?**

Seek input from the experience of others where they faced hardship whether it was by their own doing or because of other's actions. First, never be afraid to come home. This is a critical lesson from the Parable of the Prodigal Son (Luke 15). Even in situations where we bring about the hard time, we can always turn to God. We might suffer the consequences for bad choices, but God removes the eternal consequence of sin when we repent.

We should then recognize what brought us to the situation, even if it was something beyond our control or fault. Once we identify the cause, seek a solution that is in line with God's will and put it into effect as we are able. Keep focused on seeking and doing God's will throughout the situation.

## 4. How can you use this lesson to grow spiritually and help others come into a relationship with Jesus?

Although it is not a direct intent, our demonstration of faithfulness will be seen by others. It might not result in immediate appreciation, but God is aware and that's what matters the most.

We must avoid temptation. Satan knows our weaknesses and he knows how to use our strengths against us. Paul teaches us to avoid all appearances of evil (1 Thessalonians 5:22), and Peter teaches us to be alert because Satan is like a roaring lion (1 Peter 5:8).

We live on God's time. Our role is to maintain faithfulness in our service to Him (Matthew 25:14-30). In doing so, He will provide for us.

# Lesson 45 – From Prison to Prince

## Teaching Strategy

The focus of this lesson is to look at the event of Joseph's elevation to Pharaoh's court. Of special note in this lesson is how God uses faithful servants to achieve His will.

## Student Learning Outcomes

- **Know**: See how Joseph continues as a faithful servant of God in the face of trials.

- **Feel**: Appreciate that God uses our faithfulness through trials to accomplish His will.

- **Do**: Stand firm in our faith no matter the trials of life.

## Support

- Series – Genesis – Foundational Book of the Bible (Mike Mazzalongo)

- Video – Lesson 45 – From Prison to Prince

- Student Note Guide for Lesson 45

## Body of the Lesson

1.1     Pharaoh's dream
1.2     Joseph and Pharaoh
1.3     Joseph the chief official
1.4     Lessons

# Discussion Questions

Below are suggested questions to use during the guided discussion portion of the lesson. There are also suggested responses to questions to help students grasp the various concepts. These are provided to assist the discussion and are not considered as "right or wrong" responses.

## 1. What was the significance of the emblems in Pharaoh's dream from Genesis 41?

Bovine animals represented gods within Egyptian religion. Egypt was a major source of grain foods in the period. The activity of coming from the Nile is also significant as a source of water and path for trade in the region. Pharaoh recognized that this dream held great significance and perhaps, as Joseph later revealed both a threat and an opportunity.

## 2. What is the significance of Pharaoh's wise men not being able to interpret the dream but Joseph being able to?

As noted, Satan and his servants have power, but their power is not greater than God's power. Joseph credited God with the interpretation. In like fashion, we must recognize it is God's power and not ours that works for God's will.

## 3. What is noticeable about how Joseph not only provides an interpretation of the dream but that he also provides a recommendation for a wise plan of action?

God has equipped Joseph to offer an answer to Pharaoh and by also offering a solution to the situation, a demonstration of how God has provided him with the necessary wisdom. It was obviously not lost on Pharaoh as he appoints Joseph to the position he recommended. Of note is that Joseph continues to give God the credit and that he is only the willing servant.

## 4. What preparation did Joseph have to begin in his service to Pharaoh and what can we learn from this about our service to God?

Joseph had no apparent formal education to prepare him as a leader and manager for this effort. The text communicates to us that Joseph began immediately to put into action the solution God provided him. In similar fashion, we might not be formally equipped with knowledge and skills to carry out our mission to show God to the world but we should start with what we do have. God provides us with various talents and opportunities. We cannot wait until "someday" to act when we feel we have all the necessary knowledge and skill to serve the Lord in some way. We begin with what we have.

## 5. How does Joseph's rise from prison to the court of Pharaoh serve as an example of God's plans for us?

It may not be God's intention that this event in Joseph's life serve as a symbol of our reward for faithfulness, but it can serve as such.

Joseph found himself in a foreign land, forced away from family and home. He is beset by Satan testing him and through no fault of his own, he is now imprisoned. Through all of this, he remains faithful to God, even pointing to God as the source of his abilities. God was working through all of these events to bring about His will, but Joseph had to fulfill his role of seizing the moment to serve God when the opportunity presented itself.

In like fashion, we have committed our lives to God's service. Satan uses any means he can to discourage us and weaken our faith. As we continue in our faithfulness, God works His will through us and the events of our lives. In the end, as we remain faithful, He will elevate us to glory in His heavenly kingdom.

Three verses from scripture come to mind through the events of Joseph's rise from prison:

**Proverbs 22:29** – "Do you see a man skillful in his work? He will stand before kings' he will not stand before obscure men."

**Romans 8:28** – "And we know that for those who love God all things work together for good, for those who are called according to his purpose.

**2 Timothy 4:8** – "Henceforth there is laid up for me the crown of righteousness, which the Lord, the righteous judge, will award to me on that day, and not only to me but also to all who have loved his appearing."

## 6. How can you use this lesson to grow spiritually and help others come into a relationship with Jesus?

Living according to God's will includes living according to His timeline. Too often we seek our will first while seeking God's will. We want to serve God according to our will and way, and not according to His will and way.

We must remember that we are the servant. We serve humbly and allow God to reward as He chooses and when He chooses. He has promised the reward and we need to focus on faithfulness and leave the rewarding to God.

All that is good comes from God. He allows events to occur in our lives but He remains in control and seeks what is good for us. God does not bring evil, Satan does.

# Lesson 46 – Confrontation

## Teaching Strategy

The focus of this lesson is on Joseph confronting his brothers about selling him into slavery. Of special note in this lesson is how Joseph recognized God using the events of his life to bring about His will.

## Student Learning Outcomes

- **Know**: Understand how God uses events in life to bring about His will.

- **Feel**: Value the awareness of God working His will in our lives.

- **Do**: Seek to submit to God's will in our lives.

## Support

- Series – Genesis – Foundational Book of the Bible (Mike Mazzalongo)

- Video – Lesson 46 - Confrontation

- Student Note Guide for Lesson 46

## Body of the Lesson

1.1    First trip to Egypt
1.2    Second trip to Egypt
1.3    Lessons

# Discussion Questions

Below are suggested questions to use during the guided discussion portion of the lesson. There are also suggested responses to questions to help students grasp the various concepts. These are provided to assist the discussion and are not considered as "right or wrong" responses.

## 1. Summarize the events leading up to Jacob's sons traveling to Egypt and discuss observations from these events.

The intent of this question is to see how God begins to expand on the events that would culminate in the Israelites migrating to Egypt.

The significance of this is that the natural events of famine were not recognized by the general population as God working His will. Joseph understood it through Pharaoh's dreams but the population as a whole apparently did not since there is no specific mention of it.

## 2. Why would Jacob hold back Benjamin when he sent his other sons to Egypt?

It is not necessarily a weak faith in God's promise. Given the apparent death of Joseph, Jacob is reluctant to send all his sons on this journey, perhaps to ensure the continued lineage of his family.

### 3. What is significant about Reuben's charge that they were being punished for their treatment of Joseph? (Genesis 42:21-23)

They recognized their sin. Apparently, the guilt of it remained and they see the negative events in Egypt as a consequence of those long-ago actions.

### 4. How does holding Simeon in prison as a hostage relate to Joseph's treatment?

Simeon had a violent nature and was instrumental in placing Joseph in the well (pit). It was a form of imprisonment. Perhaps Joseph wished to show Simeon the impact of his previous cruelty towards himself. Also, because of his nature, Simeon had a great deal of influence over the brothers. By holding him back he was showing them their weakness in the face of his strength.

## 5. Summarize the events that required Jacob's sons to return to Egypt and discuss their significance. (Genesis 42:39-44:34)

The intent of this question is to continue to see how God works events to accomplish his will.

The significance is that now God is narrowing His focus on events. Jacob would now have to turn loose his reluctance to allow Benjamin to travel to Egypt and place a greater faith in God's promise.

## 6. How can you use this lesson to grow spiritually and help others come into a relationship with Jesus?

We might think sins are behind us. If the sin is unrepented, it will surface again in some way, perhaps in no other place than in eternity. It is critical that we guard our lives seeking to prevent sin by living faithfully before God. When we recognize sin, we must repent before God and receive His forgiveness.

Although many events in life are unpleasant, even tragic, we must continue to seek God's will during the time of these events as well as in the good times. God is the source of good and promises us His comfort.

We should develop a willingness to take the lead in obeying God and helping others as well. This was demonstrated by Judah in these series of events. He serves as an example for us in the way he persevered.

Faith involves action on our part. We must seek wisdom from God and act. In doing so, we will increase our faithfulness by allowing God to guide our actions.

# Lesson 47 – Reunion and Reconciliation

## Teaching Strategy

The focus of this lesson is Joseph's planned reunion with his father and the rest of the family. Of special note in this lesson is God's further involvement in the life of Jacob and his family to bring about His promise of a Messiah.

## Student Learning Outcomes

- **Know**: Understand the significance of the events that led the Israelite nation to relocate in Egypt.

- **Feel**: Recognize the importance of submitting to God's will and direction in all things.

- **Do**: Seek and follow God's direction in our lives.

## Support

- Series – Genesis – Foundational Book of the Bible (Mike Mazzalongo)

- Video – Lesson 47 – Reunion and Reconciliation

- Student Note Guide for Lesson 47

## Body of the Lesson

1.1    Joseph reveals himself
1.2    Joseph sends his brothers home
1.3    Israel in Egypt
1.4    Lessons

# Discussion Questions

Below are suggested questions to use during the guided discussion portion of the lesson. There are also suggested responses to questions to help students grasp the various concepts. These are provided to assist the discussion and are not considered as "right or wrong" responses.

**1. What indicators did Joseph see in his brothers that led him to feel he could reveal himself to them and how does this relate to our own repentance?**

> See text for primary indicators but encourage other insights.
>
> In similar fashion, our faith is tested. Without repentance we are unable to serve God in the way He desires. When we face our failures and put them aside, God can now reveal more of His plans for us and restore our relationship with Him.

**2. What was Joseph's attitude and spirit towards his brothers, and what can we learn from this?**

> Joseph sought to forgive and reestablish his relationship with them. He made the first move even though he was the one wronged. Rather, he used all that he had at his disposal to forgive and restore.
>
> We should adopt this same attitude. Jesus took the first step to restore us (Romans 6:8).

**3. How did Joseph's brothers' reaction to Joseph mirror our reaction to God's judgment and how can we accept God's forgiveness to lessen our fear of judgment?**

> God has promised to forgive and has forgiven us. We must accept it. We grow in this acceptance as we spiritually mature. As we grow we can't help but let go the fears attached to memories of our past sins and inadequacies.

**4. Outline the four things Joseph wanted from revealing his identity to his brothers. Which stands out to you as the most difficult and why?**

Answers will vary as to the difficult choice. Most likely forgiveness will be the most difficult.

- Ease their minds that he was no longer angry.
- Reveals how God has used this situation for good.
- Wishes to give God the glory.
- Helped them prepare for the remaining years of famine.

**5. Read Genesis 45:16-20. How does Pharaoh recognize Joseph's family and offer them everything they need from his own belongings compare to God recognizing us through Jesus and accepting us into His kingdom with all our needs met?**

Pharaoh instructs Joseph to bring his father and family to Egypt to settle in Goshen and to not worry over their possessions since he would provide everything they would need. He not only offered land, but the best of the land.

In similar fashion, Jesus will someday return and take the faithful (His family) home to God. We will be presented to God as holy and blameless and each given a place prepared specifically for us (John 14:3).

## 6. What benefits would Jacob and his family realize in moving to Egypt?

Jacob's faith in God is rewarded. His family would survive the famine. They would be living in an advanced society from which they could learn and grow into a powerful nation. They would be able to remain a pure race of God's people rather than face the issues of intermingling with pagan nations. They would draw close as a people. It would be easier to keep their religion intact.

## 7. List some observations about Joseph that show God working in his life to bring about God's will and what can we learn from this?

Answers will vary but look for indications of Joseph's faithfulness through hardships as well as good times. Sometimes we focus on faithfulness through hardships and fail to recognize that faithfulness is challenged in good times as well.

## 8. How can you use this lesson to grow spiritually and help others come into a relationship with Jesus?

- We don't' know when God is testing us or allowing us to be tested so we must be ready at all times.
- God promises to be there when we need Him. We should realize that we need Him at all times.
- We should always seek God's will in our decision making.

# Lesson 48 – Family Reunion

### Teaching Strategy

The focus of this lesson is on the final episode of Joseph's story. Of special note in this lesson is the reunion of Joseph and his family and how they settle in Egypt and God's continued faithfulness.

### Student Learning Outcomes

- **Know**: Understand the ongoing efforts of God to fulfill His promise of a Savior.

- **Feel**: Recognize God's faithfulness to His promises.

- **Do**: Live being faithful to God with confidence in His promises.

### Support

- Series – Genesis – Foundational Book of the Bible (Mike Mazzalongo)

- Video – Lesson 48 – Family Reunion

- Student Note Guide for Lesson 48

### Body of the Lesson

1.1     Jacob and Joseph meet
1.2     Jacob and the Pharaoh
1.3     The famine continues
1.4     The last days of Jacob
1.5     Jacob blesses Joseph's sons
1.6     Lessons

# Discussion Questions

Below are suggested questions to use during the guided discussion portion of the lesson. There are also suggested responses to questions to help students grasp the various concepts. These are provided to assist the discussion and are not considered as "right or wrong" responses.

**1. Summarize the reunion of Jacob and Joseph and answer the following questions.**

**What is the significance of Jacob's statement in verse 30?**

This statement could be more than just a release of sorrow to be replaced by joy. It certainly was a moment of strong emotions but there is more there that we can see. It might also be a realization of God's promise to Abraham and Jacob of making them a great nation. Jacob, now realizing that Joseph was still alive had renewed hope. Although the promised Messiah would not come through Joseph, it was evident that God was fulfilling his promise from Genesis 35:9-12.

**What is significant about Jacob's family as shepherds in Egypt?**

Egyptians despised shepherds and would not mingle with them so this would ensure they would be left alone by the Egyptians and allowed to flourish as a nation. It would also ensure that the people would not intermarry with the Egyptians. Goshen was also good land to raise livestock.

**2. What is significant about the use of the word "sojourn" in Genesis 47:4?**

Sojourn is a term meaning to travel through. They recognized that this land was a temporary dwelling. They retained hope to return to their own land someday.

In similar fashion, as citizens of God's Kingdom on earth we are sojourners traveling through this life on our way to the promised land of being with God in eternity.

### 3. Summarize the interaction between Jacob and Pharaoh from Genesis 47:7-10 and discuss its significance.

Joseph presents his father to Jacob. Pharaoh had already blessed Jacob by allowing his family to live in Goshen and to provide them with what they needed. He now asks Jacob about his life perhaps recognizing the spiritual depth of Jacob's nature. Jacob blesses Pharaoh as both a way to thank God for using Pharaoh to bless his family, and to honor and thank Pharaoh for his hospitality. The interaction between these two leaders was an interaction between a political giant and a spiritual giant. Yet again, we see God using circumstances to further His will for Jacob.

### 4. What is significant about how the famine continuing and its impact on the world of the day, and how does this relate to Paul's teachings in Romans 13?

God stated that the famine would continue for seven years. God places leaders in positions of authority to rule and perform justice for all under their authority. Paul teaches us we are to honor our governing authorities since they are given their power by God.

Another note worthy of discussion is how God's people flourished in Goshen while others came to rely on Pharaoh. This shows God's blessings on His people.

## 5. Why would Jacob insist on his body being returned to Canaan?

This was the land God had promised him. Jacob had already referred to himself as a sojourner meaning this separation from his true homeland was temporary. He was doing his part to fulfil God's promise of a land for his people. This was a final act of faith. It was also a way of tying the people back to Canaan even though they would physically remain in Egypt for another 400 years.

## 6. Summarize Jacob's blessings on his sons from Genesis 48.

Jacob reminds them of God's promise. He now transfers that promise to his sons. He also establishes the tribes of Israel named after his sons (verse 6).

## 7. How can you use this lesson to grow spiritually and help others come into a relationship with Jesus?

God will always work His will. We evaluate life from our own perspective and sometimes don't see it from God's view. We must work to develop an understanding of God working through our lives.

God will bless us no matter the situation we are in. Again, we have a view of the immediate rather than the eternal.

It is a difficult lesson for us to learn that God is always in control, especially during difficult times. As we grow spiritually, we will see more of God's work. This serves to strengthen our faith.

# Lesson 49 – Jacob's Prophecies

## Teaching Strategy

The focus of this lesson is to review the closing actions of Jacob and Joseph's life. Of special note in this lesson is how we can look at their lives as examples of faith in action.

## Student Learning Outcomes

- **Know**: Understand God's actions to maintain His faithfulness to His promise of a Messiah.

- **Feel**: Appreciate God's faithfulness.

- **Do**: Seek to live faithfully to God's will.

## Support

- Series – Genesis – Foundational Book of the Bible (Mike Mazzalongo)

- Video – Lesson 49 – Jacob's Prophecies

- Student Note Guide for Lesson 49

## Body of the Lesson

1.1    Jacob's prophecy concerning the future of his sons
1.2    Jacob's last words and burial
1.3    Joseph's death
1.4    Lessons

# Discussion Questions

Below are suggested questions to use during the guided discussion portion of the lesson. There are also suggested responses to questions to help students grasp the various concepts. These are provided to assist the discussion and are not considered as "right or wrong" responses.

**1. Summarize the prophecy of each of Jacob's sons and answer the following questions.**

**Why would Jacob prophesy concerning his sons?**

It was a way to provide them with direction and perhaps encouragement and warning for their lives.

**Speculate. Could the sons change the direction of their lives as given by Jacob, and if so, what would be required of them, and how does this impact us individually as God's people?**

It is possible that they could change their lives. Someone once said we are the sum of all of our decisions and certainly some of Jacob's sons had chosen to take a path in life contrary to God's will. Yet God also gives us the ability to choose. If we see that our lives are not going in a direction God wills, then we should take action to change the direction. We have to deal with the consequences of bad choices, but we can also resolve to not repeat those actions. This is at the heart of our repentance as we strive to please the Lord.

**2. Why did Jacob specify where he was to be buried?**

He was ensuring that he would be returned to the land promised by God. This closed the life that at times was marked by weak faith but in the end, Jacob put into place actions indicating his obedience to God.

### 3. What is significant about Joseph's brothers fearing that Joseph would take vengeance on them now that Jacob was dead?

Perhaps they were looking at the situation from how they would have reacted. They did not recognize, even after all this time, that Joseph was not a vengeful man and that he had indeed forgiven them. Joseph recognized that the actions they had taken had actually allowed God's will to occur (vs 20).

### 4. What was significant about Joseph desiring to be buried in Canaan?

It was a statement of faith that God would fulfil His promise of a land for Israel. His faith was strong enough that he wanted to be buried with his ancestors and those who would come after him.

## 5. How can you use this lesson to grow spiritually and help others come into a relationship with Jesus?

We sometimes look at life from the perspective of what is happening in the moment and not recognizing God working His will over our lifetime. This is seen in the many lives of the characters in Genesis. We must deal with the immediate, but we should also keep an eye on the larger picture of a lifetime of service to God.

If someone has not begun their life journey under God's will, then now is the moment to change their direction. As Paul would state in Philippians 3:13-14, "Brothers and sisters, I do not consider myself yet to have taken hold of it. But one thing I do: forgetting what is behind and straining toward what is ahead, I press on toward the goal to win the prize for which God has called me heavenward in Christ Jesus." (ESV)

# Lesson 50 – Final Summary

### Teaching Strategy

The focus of this lesson is to review the closing actions of Jacob and Joseph's life. Of special note in this lesson is to how we can look at their lives as examples of faith in action.

### Student Learning Outcomes

- **Know**: Understand the overall message of Genesis
- **Feel**: Appreciate God's faithfulness to His promises.
- **Do**: Seek to live faithfully to God's will.

### Support

- Series – Genesis – Foundational Book of the Bible (Mike Mazzalongo)
- Video – Lesson 50 – Final Summary
- Student Note Guide for Lesson 50

### Body of the Lesson

1.1    Overall message of Genesis
1.2    Lessons

## Discussion Questions

Below are suggested questions to use during the guided discussion portion of the lesson. There are also suggested responses to questions to help students grasp the various concepts. These are provided to assist the discussion and are not considered as "right or wrong" responses.

## 1. Summarize Genesis in one sentence.

Look for expressions such as God's faithfulness, love, power, influence, etc.

## 2. What are the major lessons you have learned from Genesis?

Refer to the text for suggested responses.

## 3. What are some major expressions of faith described in Genesis and what do they teach us?

Answers will vary but look for responses concerning how the major characters of Genesis took actions according to God's will when they did not understand why or how to act.

Faith is not something new. We can see how the characters from Genesis had to have faith. Sometimes their faith was not strong yet God still worked through them.

We frequently don't know how to act according to God's will, or our faith is weak. We can learn from the actions of the characters in Genesis that we should seek God's wisdom to make decisions according to God's will. Also, realize that God knows and works with our weaknesses. He seeks faithfulness not perfection.

**4. Read James 1:1-8 and discuss how this passage relates to the overall life of the major characters in Genesis.**

God had a plan for man's salvation, even before we sinned. This is a tremendous indicator of His love for us. He created us, knows us and still loves us. When we're strong we must recognize that it is God's power working in us and give Him the glory. When we are weak, we must seek His forgiveness and strength with the faith that He will provide it.

The major characters of Genesis, specifically Abraham, Isaac, Jacob and Joseph each had moments of both weakness and strength. In the end they recognized God working in their lives and fulfilled their destiny according to His will. James reminds us that God has promised us salvation. James states that we will face trials but that we should look at these as opportunities to build faith. We must also know that when things seem to be going well, it is a chance to build strength and use those moments to glorify God.

A champion runner knows that instead of coasting or easing up in the drive towards the finish line when the way is smooth, level or downhill, he should instead increase the drive towards the finish line. The time to coast is after the race.

In similar ways, we sometimes there have the tendency to "coast" through the good times in life and not recognize them as a gift from God. We should increase our service and praise to God during the good times so that our faith will be sustained in the challenging times.

In all things, no matter the situation, we give God the glory.